FARMSTAND

VEGETABLES

TRADITIONAL COUNTRY LIFE RECIPE SERIES

FARMSTAND
VEGETABLES

by *Jane Wilson Morton & Marianne K. Preston*

Interior Illustrations
Jane Lawrence

Cover Illustration
Lisa Adams

The Brick Tower Press ®
1230 Park Avenue, New York, NY 10128
Copyright © 2002
by Jane Wilson Morton & Marianne K. Preston
All rights reserved under the International and Pan-American Copyright Conventions.
Printed in the United States by J. T. Colby & Company, Inc., New York.
No part of this publication may be reproduced, stored in a retrieval system, or transmitted in any form or by any means, electronic, mechanical, photocopying, recording, or otherwise, without the prior written permission of the publisher.

Morton, Jane Wilson & Preston, Marianne K.
The Traditional Country Life Recipe Series:
Includes Index
ISBN 1-883283-21-3, softcover

Library of Congress Catalog Card
Number: 2001 132548
First Edition, October 2002

TABLE OF CONTENTS

ACKNOWLEDGMENTS

The following individuals and establishments have graciously shared information and expertise with us. We wish to thank them and recognize their contributions for without their sharing, we would be unable to truly understand the essence of a farmstand.

Domaine Chandon Restaurant and Chef Robert Curry—One California Drive, Yountville, Ca. 94599.

Augusta Field—1921 Roanoke Avenue, Riverhead, NY 11901.

Florida Tomato Committee—4401 East Colonial Drive Orlando, Fl. 32803.

Mildred Greaney—granddaughter of farmer John Filasky, New Hyde Park, NY.

Hallockville Family Farm Museum—Sound Avenue, Hallockville, NY.

Monica and Ed Harbes—Harbes Farmstand, POB 1524, Mattituck, NY 11952.

Louise Hansen—Katy, Tx.—Texas farmstands.

Janie Kirk—the Kentucky Soybean Association.

Mary Kaye Merwin—formerly with the Cornell Cooperative Extension of Nassau County, NY.

Robert Mondavi Online Newsletter—Napa Valley Farmers' Markets, Ca.

Terry and Peter Meyers—Meyers Farm, Woodbury Road, Woodbury, NY.

Roy Lee Neill—great-grandson of founder of Neill's Tomato Farm, Fort Pierce, Fl.

The Plimoth Plantation—Plymouth, Ma.—Indian farming.

Lolly and Jake Rottkamp—Fox Hollow Farm Stand, 2287 Sound Avenue, Calverton, NY 11933—a Long Island farm family.

Karen and Fred Lee—Sang Lee Farms, 25180 County Road 48, Peconic, NY 11958–specialty greens.

Starpoli Family, especially Maureen at Red Oaks Mills Farm, NY— a farm family saga.

Suffolk County Historical Society—300 West Main Street, Riverhead, NY 11901—Long Island farm history.

Paula Youngs Weir and Jo-Hana Youngs Gooth—Youngs Farm, the Annex, Hegeman's Lane, Old Brookville, NY 11545.

FARMSTAND
"Eat your vegetables!"

One of the greatest impacts on vegetable consumption in the past 20 years has been the astounding popularity of the greenmarkets and farmers' markets that are proliferating in cities and towns and villages. Greenmarkets are the 21st century versions of the legendary farmstand—and farmstands are legendary as we found when we started looking into the history of farming and the selling of fresh produce. The growth of urbanization from 1810 transformed the colonial farm from self-sufficiency to a market enterprise. As the country expanded westward by canals and railroads, Eastern and Middle Atlantic farmers concentrated more on dairying and "truck farming" as beef and pork and cotton production moved west and south. Supplying major and secondary cities became a major source of income for many New England and Middle Atlantic farmers.[1]

As a way to prevent disease and maintain good health, vegetables also provide wonderful amenities—their vibrant colors—red, green, yellow, orange, purple, and white, enhance many a plate. They also provide interesting flavor and texture contrasts.

When you are selecting vegetables for a menu, remember to consider the combinations of color, flavor, texture, and shape that provide the eye and flavor appeal that will tempt a diner's palate. Hopefully the recipes in this book will inspire you not only to "eat your veggies" but to "love your veggies."

We would like to think that this farmstand vegetable cookbook will encourage you to seek out a farmstand in your own home town and, when traveling in a rural or urban area, to stop at a farmstand or greenmarket. Take time to talk to the stand owner, learn about the different varieties of vegetables he offers and how to prepare them. You might just find yourself chatting with the produce grower, gaining useful information about the produce you are buying and then even sharing a recipe or two. Enjoy the ambiance of the farmstand and give a thought to the needs, the toil and the entrepreneurship that brought the legendary farmstand to the position it holds today, for it is a small but very integral part of our American history.

A FARMSTAND MEMORY
by Jane Wilson Morton

It was in the Adirondack Mountains of upstate New York in an old resort and children's camp town called Schroon Lake that I had my first experience with farm fresh. I was 3 1/2 and our family was spending a few weeks at an ageing farm. There were lots of little pigs, creamy milk still warm from the cow, and very little indoor plumbing. One day I was out in a field and dropped a rock on my toe. I cried uncontrollably and hysterically as only a 3 1/2 year old can. Everyone tried to comfort my pain but it was the elderly farmer who managed to get me to smile. He presented me with a huge red ripe strawberry fresh

from the strawberry patch. It was succulent and delicious and unlike any I'd ever eaten. Many years later I spent a lovely June afternoon picking strawberries with a friend at a U-pick strawberry farm. One of the berries looked too good to resist and I popped it into my mouth. Still slightly warm from the afternoon sun, it was so perfect I doubt I will ever duplicate the taste sensation. It was the epitome of farmstand fresh.

Actually, the quest for the sweetest, most tender corn- on-the-cob is my earliest memory of farmstand shopping. Of course, my grandfather's garden corn, picked just before cooking, couldn't have been fresher but was limited in quantity as he only had a small backyard plot. Long Island, all 105 miles of it, had many farms and its produce fed much of New York City. However, excess produce and some of the items grown in smaller amounts showed up at stands, usually along the most well-traveled thoroughfares.

When word got around that a particular stand had great corn, the discriminating corn lover headed there for his share of the delicious sunny kernels. It was important to know just when the day's pick arrived at the stand so you could have your choice of perfect ears. One would not want to arrive and find them sold out, either. We ate our fill, often fighting over who would get the last ear on the platter. Dripping with butter and sprinkled lightly with salt (or sugar), I was content making a meal of corn alone.

My Aunt Hannah introduced me to farmstand shopping when I was about 10. Her husband was very particular about all his food and demanded the best. He grew his own blueberries and the gardener had to treat them with kid gloves. We would drive several towns away to the best stand for fresh vegetables. The local growing season had miraculously spewed forth gorgeous red tomatoes, bright bunches of greens, all kinds of squashes, peppers, cucumbers, cauliflower, scallions, radishes, and potatoes, along with the corn. My grandmother loved to prepare a huge vegetable salad with as many as 12 or 13 garden vegetables in it. What a way to eat your "five-a-day."

I've watched as farm stands and farms close to make way for million-dollar homes and housing developments and weep a little as each one goes. Somehow, many manage to remain and thrive and it's still exciting to see the sign that reads. "Local corn is in." You buy your first dozen or half dozen of the season, rush home, cook them, brush the golden kernels with melted butter, and take that first bite. Are they even better than ever or are they just appreciated more?

A FARMSTAND MEMORY
by Marianne K. Preston

Certain wonderful childhood memories stay and tend to become more vivid as time passes. My farmstand memories go back to the 1940s, when I spent my summers on Aunt Sarah and Uncle Tony's farm in Wappinger Falls, New York. My farm experience with them remains as fresh in my mind as if it had occurred just last week. This was where I learned that a watermelon seed, when planted, grows and becomes a watermelon. A revelation as my daily turf consisted of the concrete and asphalt of Greenwich Village.

I would visit their farm for a month or so each summer and each day would begin with an unwelcome awakening at 4:30 AM, to ride in the back of an old pickup truck, sipping hot coffee, and munching on crusty bread. We would drive to Wappinger Falls and pick up the local pickers who waited on the dark corner in a silent town with a predawn backdrop.

We were on our way from the warm homestead on the outer fringes of Poughkeepsie, actually in back of the then small but exclusive women's college, Vassar, to the farm. We picked strawberries, raspberries, and currants, and seasonal vegetables under a hot, dry sun. The pay was five cents for a half pint of raspberries and ten cents for a quart of strawberries, the going rate paid to each picker. I earned the same as everyone else, even though I was "the farmer's niece." My bonus was that occasionally I was allowed to work in the receiving shack and check in the fruit as the pickers brought in their loads. Seasonal vegetables and some fruit were brought to farmstands in the area and sold to the local residents while the bulk was sent on to my uncle's distribution area, then called the Washington Market, located in downtown Poughkeepsie. Not everyone had access to a car in those rural areas so folks walked to the farmstand for the produce of the day.

My father's family wanted him to join the farm, and we did spend a summer there to test it out, but my father remained a city person. He was brought up on this farm and perhaps his memories were not as pleasant or as romanticized as mine. He preferred city life and so we stayed on in Greenwich Village.

The Village at that time was a haven for writers and artists and the immigrant families that created ethnic neighborhoods. My Italian grandmother lived on Bleecker Street and it was there that I experienced what might be described as the farmstands of the city. They were pushcarts, just off the street curbs, loaded down with produce that came from upstate farms. Each pushcart was overflowing with the plumpest of eggplant, the ripest of tomatoes, lush heads of escarole, and crisp heads of lettuce. Like the rural farmstands, crudely printed signs told you the prices and freshness was never a question. Along with the sales you were liable to hear a recipe or two or a family argument. Like the rural farmstands, you knew the vendors and made small talk and exchanged pleasantries. It was another part of farmstand history.

FARMSTAND HISTORY
"Farmstand!"

The word alone recaptures a feeling, an atmosphere, a warm colorful seasonal memory. Who among us has not driven by a tottering, handmade contraption of a farmstand—loaded down with sultry red tomatoes, bright green asparagus stalks, a row of snow white cauliflower heads, intriguing stalks of brussels sprouts, bins of pale green corn husks—and not been tempted to stop. For extra added color and attraction, gigantic bunches of anemones, gladiolus, statice or other flowers add to the lure of the farmstand. In fact the more rickety the stand, the more chance of stopping in hopes that this farmer and his crop will provide us with the freshest of edibles, the lowest of prices, and as a bonus, if you've a mind to listen, the most homespun of rural chatter. This is the ambiance of the farmstand.

But what exactly is a "farmstand"? Or should it be "farm stand"? The dictionary lists no such word as "farmstand" but the aesthetics of the words joined as one have led these authors to take license and follow their feelings. Therefore, for the purposes of this book we write of the farmstand as one word. Treating the words as one seems to be in harmony with the concept of the togetherness in the old farming family.

Farmstands with produce for sale still abound in this country, especially where crops are plentiful and farms are still a family affair. Selling crops on the road or in front of a homestead seems to be the simplest approach to utilizing excess crops, avoiding waste, sharing the bounty of one's expertise, and earning added income. Farm wives canned and dried extra fruits and vegetables for use during the coming year. At times they sold some of their preserves at the farmstand. Certainly they entered the most flavorful and attractive jars in the state or

County Fair, hoping for a blue ribbon which was, and still is, a sure lure for the farmstand shopper. It was an early form of public relations and advertising.

Some folks look at the farmstand simply as a place to buy the freshest of produce for the least amount of money, but in fact there was a time when farmstands were social connectors. They provided affable communal relationships and business interactions. Small and personal, they also created a sense of identity and  place, and told a story about the inhabitants of a town. The farmstand provided an education to travelers by letting them know what a particular area was producing, suggesting a climate and soil type. Today, in the northeast, a farmstand displaying a fall harvest of pumpkin, turnip, and squash, heads of broccoli, cabbage, and kale makes heads turn and cars stop.

Farmers often preferred bartering to selling and while some of their produce would stay on their own farms for trading with neighbors and those passing by, many farmers drove all night to greet the dawn at what were known as "middle-of-the-street-markets." These were markets formed in the middle of large open areas to access wares from all sides. Along with sales there was a great deal of trading between the farmers; a bushel of my corn for a bushel of your tomato. As transportation modes improved and people had greater mobility these markets disappeared and became the large, open avenues we now find in cities like Philadelphia, New York, and Boston. These "middle-of-the-street-markets" were the forerunners of what are now our city greenmarkets, such as New York City's Union Square Greenmarket. [2]

Conversations about farmstands with people in various areas of the United States reveal many similarities as well as some differences. For example, Mary

Kaye Merwin, a former Director of the Cooperative Extension on Long Island (New York), grew-up on a farm in Wisconsin. Her father worked many acres of corn and soybeans but the corn wasn't sweet table corn. It was commercial field corn. By comparison, on Long Island and in New Jersey, the farms are much smaller and the corn grown is more likely to be all sweet table corn. However, Mary Kaye further related that her dad always planted the two outside rows of

the cornfield with sweet table corn. This fed family, friends and neighbors. Neighbors, in turn, traded back other commodities. A lot of this bartering was based on frugality. Nobody wanted to see good food wasted. Trading also provided variety. Any home gardener knows that when the tomatoes or zucchini start ripening the crop is usually an abundant one and there is plenty for sharing.

Farmer Merwin also reserved a portion of his fields near the road for two spring crops—rhubarb and asparagus. As it turned he selected the wrong area for such an alluring crop. On warm spring days, vacationers visiting that part of Wisconsin from nearby Chicago saw the tempting stalks near the road and assumed they were theirs for the picking. The family never had a farmstand but Mary Kaye pointed out that the easiest way to sell any excess produce was to hook up a tractor to a farm wagon full of fresh vegetables and pull it to a busy road or corner.

From the 1700s through the 1940s and 50s there were fresh vegetable vendors, who, after picking up their produce from a central market, plied their wares from pushcarts along the curbs of city roads. These areas were not called greenmarkets then, but they were surely the precursors of things to come. Some vendors who started with a horse and buggy progressed to little trucks with open sides where fresh produce was displayed. The homemakers came out as the produce seller called, "Fresh vegetables for sale."

According to Eric Sloane's *America Yesterday*, in the 1700s and 1800s these vendors were called "professional criers" and were considered the vaudevillians of their day. Sociable chatter was encouraged and it took place with the vendor and other neighbors along with the purchase of the day's vegetables and fruits. Electric refrigeration only became widespread in the 1930s. Shopping for food was done on a daily basis as it is still done today in many European cities. Julia Child loves to tell about her kitchen facilities in Paris when she lived there and worked on her first book. She had no refrigeration but in winter, of course, there was always the window sill. In New York City during the 1920s, construction of new tenement buildings included a "produce-box," open to the outside by several small holes for cold air, but accessible from the inside like a tin box imbedded in the kitchen wall.

Many city kids, too, had their experiences and memories of various versions of farmstands for there were vegetable vendors in every neighborhood. Their experiences started when their mothers sent them for small purchases with a strict admonition about the quality they must demand. The order might have been for "fifteen-cents-worth-of-soup-greens." And with that exact amount of money in hand they trusted the vendor to give them their moneys worth (unless they dropped a dime on the way).

The type of produce offered by these various vendors also depended on the nationality of the vendor. In Greenwich Village in New York City the vendors on Bleecker Street were primarily Italian and the vegetables sold concentrated on those used in Italian cooking—eggplant, escarole, Swiss chard, garlic and broccoli rabe. That is not to say that these ingredients were not used in other types of ethnic cooking. The items sold in New York's Chinatown reflected the demands of the Chinese population. These markets sold vegetables like bok choy, ginger root, Chinese eggplant, and water chestnuts. Part of the life experience of growing up in the city was the varied ethnicity of neighborhoods and the diversity of the type of foods each nationality offered. Sociologically the exposure to the different ethnicities in big cities, with their food and their markets, gave city kids a broadening experience, likely one of which they were totally unaware.

The lay of the land and the accessibility to water had, and still has, a great deal to do with the survival of farms. Once farmers installed sprinkling systems and irrigation, crops were more consistent. It was at the Schumacher Farm in New Hyde Park, Long Island in 1936 that the first portable irrigation system was installed. The Portable Overhead Irrigation system was popularly demonstrated on Long Island, New York in 1937. Today, all the good farmland on Long Island's east end is irrigated. Increased knowledge about the control of insects and plant diseases, availability of better seeds, fertilizers, and pesticides also increased crop yields.

Acquaintances in Utah and Arizona reveal that farmstands are disappearing as housing developments spring up. "Oh," they'll say, "we used to have fruit stands

or vegetable stands but they've disappeared." Farming, after all, is hard work, and Mother Nature isn't always kind in her distribution of the best weather for good crop production and in some years the crop can be very lean.

The Rio Grand Valley in South Texas is a major producer of many crops which are sent all over the United States. Katy is a town on Route 10 which goes from Houston to San Antonio. Its 1990 census population was a little over 8000. Louise Hansen who lives in Katy, reports that there are lots of individual vegetable and melon farmers who set up shop wherever they think they can sell their crops. Some use the backs of their trucks, some park on the roadside and put their wares in baskets, others have crude structures which are permanent but only used when their produce is ripe. "The consumer just can't depend on these sellers to be there on the day the product is needed," she says.

In San Jose, the doorstep of the nation's salad bowl, there are still may farmstands. Driving through that part of the country and seeing miles of greens growing is a sight to behold. One town, Watsonville, is the artichoke capital of the world. Gilroy is the garlic capital. A tour of a garlic farm revealed that there are infinite varieties of garlic. The sideline of one farm included making and bottling its own garlicky salsa. There was also a gift shop devoted to everything garlic. The Napa Valley, home of some of the best California wines, features wonderful farmers' markets rather than individual farmstands. Many of the area chefs and entire classes of students from the Culinary Institute of America at Greystone spend the morning shopping for the freshest seasonal bounty.

FARMSTANDS AND THE FAMILY
Who staffs the farmstand?

Family members staff the farmstand. They have always been an integral part of farming and many a farmstand started with a form of childhood entrepreneurship. A son or daughter sold leftover produce from a roughly made stand or cart on the front lawn. Over time the stand sometimes progressed into a thriving business with mom assisting in arranging vegetables and adding flowers from her garden to entice passersby into stopping.

When Paula Youngs Weir and her sister Jo-Hana Youngs Gooth were in third and fifth grades respectively, they asked their father, a farmer, if they could sell the excess produce left over from the market truck. They wanted to set up their business in front of the farmhouse. He said they could, for one day. That one day stretched into the whole summer and the girls made an astounding one-thousand dollars. The next year, their father mowed down a two-hundred-year-old carriage shed to build a farmstand for the family. Today, these sisters run one of most upscale farmstands on Long Island (New York) with a summer staff of over ten. The stand is the sole outlet for the seventeen-acre-farm's produce. However, they also sell homemade pies, soups, jams, cookies, and breads along with fresh herb plants. The pie sales surpass the vegetable sales, they say. When asked for a favorite vegetable recipe, Paula immediately volunteered her favorite, creamed kohlrabi. (See page 67.) She also volunteered a favorite way to use the knobby celeriac root. Peel, cook, and purée it in with mashed potatoes, with a three-to-two ratio of potato to celeriac. "It's yummy," she says.

Monica and Edward Harbes' farm nestles on one-hundred acres on the eastern north fork of Long Island. They are parents to eight children, all involved in the farm and the farmstand. Edward Harbes had worked with his father farming Long Island potatoes. After a period of time he realized that potatoes might not be something he wanted to grow on a long-term basis, but he did recall growing small patches of a sweet corn as a young boy. He looked into the prospects of turning the soil over to corn and checked out a new super-sweet corn, a variety that he did not think was being grown in commercial quantities on Long Island. The super-sweet corn has a higher sugar content and it converts to starch more slowly. Regular corn should be eaten the same day while the super-sweet variety can be kept under refrigeration for several days and still retain good flavor and texture.

In 1989, he was ready to sell his super-sweet variety. Along with son Jason, then about ten, he started to build a 14x14-foot gazebo. The building did not proceed that quickly and Jason spent much of his time asking, "Is it ready yet?" The corn was ready, Jason was ready, the gazebo was not quite ready. Appreciating his sons' enthusiasm, Edward set up a 4x4-foot bin under a large maple tree. The corn sold quickly and a farmstand was born—the first of three.

West of the Harbes' farm rests Briermere Farm, a landmark, first purchased in 1902 by a New York State experimental station agent from Geneva, New York. The farmstand's produce still remains a major attraction with the added allure of some of the best homemade fruit pies in the state. They have their own fruit orchards and during the summer and during the holidays, folks stand in line to buy Briermere s baked goods.

Janie Kirk works for the Kentucky Soybean Board in Princeton, Kentucky, and grew up in a Kentucky farm family with six children. Their father gave them a piece of the farm to work as their own corn patch. They had to prepare the soil, plant the seed, weed the area, and harvest the corn. Then they could sell it for their own profit. This was a great way for kids to learn entrepreneurship. "Things have changed greatly here in Kentucky," Janie said. "There used to be lots of farmstands compared to the few around today." Farmstand selling has been curtailed by stricter regulations from the Department of Health as well as a requirement for more detailed record keeping for tax purposes. Many farmers find this too demanding. The Department of Agriculture has sponsored farmers' markets across the state by paying the rent on the space used. Farmers can bring their produce to this area to sell. Although Janie said that things are different today, she did note that the major Kentucky farmstand veggies are still corn, tomatoes, and green beans with pumpkins in the fall, but watermelon and cantaloupe are two of the state's most popular crops. "Unless you can get into a family farm, it's tough to be a farmer now," she said.

In the1930s the Starpoli family began a farmstand and farm family saga that has extended over seventy years. It is an example of how a farmstand is born, develops, and maintains itself for several generations through cooperation and involvement of family members. The saga began when Tony Starpoli and his son, Moe, opened a produce market or what we would now call a greenmarket, on Main Street in Poughkeepsie, New York—the lush Hudson Valley area of the state.

Moe's daughter, Maureen, now living in Florida recalls, "My dad would take a late train, every night, to the New York City Washington Growers' Market to purchase produce and fruits to be shipped to Poughkeepsie the next day for sale to local stores." As she tells it, "He would return home at four or five in the morning, consume a hearty breakfast, head to bed for a few hours sleep and then go to the Washington Market (the local version of the New York City market.) for a full days' work."

In the mid 1940s Tony Starpoli started their first farm in Wappinger Falls, New York. Moe continued to run the market and while much of the produce from the farm—tomatoes, fruits, and lettuce went directly to the Washington Market some was left for the farmstand in Wappinger Falls. Pickers came from the local area and the farmstand was manned by the family. Niece and author, Marianne K. Preston, helped out on the stand when she made her summer trips to Poughkeepsie and now treasures her childhood experience.

As the Washington Market grew, partners from outside the family were taken in but the family's involvement never diminished. Tony's daughter, Lucy, became the bookkeeper. Sons and daughters, aunts and uncles, and in-laws were always participants. At one point the family owned three farms; the Stanfordville Farm, the Cornell Farm, and the Red Oaks Mill Farm. When Tony died, Moe closed the market and took over the farms' farmstands. They were eventually sold and the last farmstand located in Red Oaks Mills and run by Chris Starpoli was sold in 2000. Moe Starpoli, up until the time he died in 1998 at age 85, managed to retain a commanding presence at the Red Oaks Mill farmstand. He would sit on a stool, cane in hand, under the protection of a large shed and direct the harvesting of corn, basil, and tomatoes. These were truly farms and farmstands run by family. With the selling of this last Starpoli bastion, Maureen Starpoli reminisced, "I am very proud and even more than that, grateful for all their efforts, their long hours of sweat and the work. We have been blessed to have known and shared such quality time with them all."

From Florida, we learned the history of Neill's Tomato Farmstand in Fort Pierce, off route I-95, as reported by Roy Neill, the great-grandson of the farm's founder. It was started in the 1940s post World War II era, when major farm systems were established in St. Lucie, Palm Beach, and Dade Counties. It wasn't until the 1960s that small local farmstands came into being. The farms produced two to three pickings a year and the vegetables, mainly tomatoes, were sent to the packing houses. After the pickings were completed, the farms allowed hucksters to come in and pick the remaining vegetables. The hucksters, (defined in the dictionary as peddlers,) in this instance paid the farmer by the crate, and loaded their trucks with the produce. After the hucksters picked their loads, they would go to markets to resell their crates to farmstand vendors who in turn loaded the vegetables in trucks and sold them at roadside stands.

Once the farmers realized how much was to be made with the leftover crops, they decided to cash in on the idea. The Neills came up with the idea of "U-Pick" Farmstands. The first U-Pick was opened about 1975 by Roy Lee Neill and his son, David, of Fort Pierce. The main crop is tomatoes, but they also grow squash and peppers, greens, beans and okra. If the crop is unusually high, the farmer will pick some himself to sell at the stand. "Customers enjoy picking their own," the farmers say. "It gives them a down-home feeling." The large Neill commercial farm ships tomatoes all over the world and many family members work at the farm and farmstands.

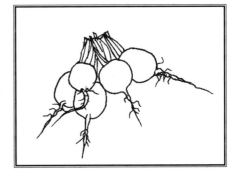

As the new century begins, Neill's Farm is working five-hundred acres, growing primarily tomatoes. They have now added artichokes to their farmstand items and the sight of a field of artichoke bushes, in this Florida community, commands attention with their tall stalks and dramatic crown.

THE SAGA OF A FARM FAMILY
The Rottkamps

When your ancestors emigrated to America in the mid 1800s from Germany, and today your branch of the family numbers over two-thousand, and many have been farmers through the years, you indeed come from a farm family. The Rottkamp family has regular reunions and whole albums have been published with many wedding pictures and the names of everyone catalogued into their proper lineage.

Jake (Jacob) and Lolly (really Carmen) Rottkamp are carrying on the family farming tradition with two-hundred-fifty acres on Long Island's north fork. They own thirty-five acres and lease the rest. Their son Jeff, who lives next door, loves to farm and owns forty acres. Their daughter took an alternate route and become a tractor mechanic. Jeff's two sons also pitch in at the farm.

Lolly, who got her nickname because she loved lollipops as a child, grew up on a Long Island farm and became a nurse, married a farmer, and returned to the farm life she enjoyed. It was Rottkamp family farmland that was sold to become Levittown, New York, the community that materialized after World War II to help house returning veterans. Lolly's grandparents' farm in Northport was sold to the Rottkamp family who later sold the property for development. The old barn remained until the summer of 2000 when a fire destroyed everything but the framework. A couple of old Rottkamp farm houses still remain standing near Levittown.

"Fox Hollow Farm Stand" identifies the Rottkamp stand. The name stems from seeing foxes romp out in their fields for years. Originally, potatoes were their mainstay crop and the stand was opened their first summer (1967) to provide added income. Today, sweet corn is their premier summer crop with a field of strawberries and one of rhubarb in the spring. There are droves of pumpkins, squash, and gourds in the fall. Tomatoes, too, are an important crop. Plants are cultivated from seed in their greenhouse.

With his blue eyes twinkling, Jake explained that corn matures in sixty-eight to seventy-eight days, depending on Mother Nature. "Father time is a male and you can always count on him to be dependable but Mother Nature, being female, can be very fickle," he said. The Rottkamps have a large wholesale business and their corn shows up at many other smaller stands. Cauliflower, once a huge crop on Long Island, is no longer important with the advent of year round supplies from California and other states. "When you're a farmer," the Rottkamps say, "you have to be a botanist, a chemist, a mechanic, a carpenter, and a weather man," a regular jack of all trades.

THE LOOK OF A FARMSTAND
"...probably an old cart..."

Many a farmstand started as something for the farm children to do to give them a sense of productivity and family partnership. The look of the farmstand might have been very artless in that it was probably an old cart or maybe vegetable crates piled and slanted so that the items looked fresh and inviting. Somewhere else it might have been the addition of a shed or an overhead awning of some kind. Some stands remain in their original condition and were never improved while others became small showplaces with beautifully arranged vegetables, orderly signs, computerized scales, and cash registers. Occasionally these stands became large marketplaces that included dried flowers, fresh flowers, wall displays of herbs, colorful posters, jam, jellies, and herbal vinegars. These are the farmstands that became signposts of an era and are still a stabilizing force in a community.

In this century of beautiful people our veggies have to look beautiful too and this makes the look of the farmstand very important. While one driver may seek out a flower bedecked farmstand worthy of a photo opportunity, another driver may prefer an old-fashioned, crudely constructed farmstand. The appearance of the farmstand steadily changes but hopefully there will always be the makeshift stand that lends itself to a quick setup and teardown and the simple stand that trails the back of a pickup truck or the pickup truck itself .

Above and beyond the farm family's own consumption, extra produce, if not sold from a home farmstand, could be loaded on the back of the most basic of farmstands—the farm wagon. Pulled by tractor to a desirable side-of-the-road location, the products would lure passers by. Often an "honor box" would be placed conveniently, with change in it, for payment by the buyer—on his honor! There are still farms that adhere to this method of money exchange. There are still farmers with faith in the consumer. A farmer's time is valuable and how he uses it depends on what Mother Nature deals out to him. He cannot afford to sit in front of a field of strawberries and wait until inexperienced sightseers pick their pint and pay the fee. He would rather have trust that the majority will do the right thing.

THE 21st CENTURY FARMSTAND
"Where have all the Farmstands gone?"

Americans are in the midst of a love affair with vegetables and the best place to find the freshest of vegetables is at a farmstand, whether it be on a busy road or a quiet country lane. The farmstand had and still has much allure in the 21st century. They have never really been out of style but in the past 10 years farmstands have blossomed from simple racks of produce to small, barn style structures with displays of produce to rival any of our cities' greatest supermarkets. The benefactor of all this abundance is the lucky consumer who can take advantage of the vegetable season in a relaxed atmosphere, whether on vacation or not. Good cooks and discriminating consumers have always demanded the freshest, choicest, most succulent produce. Many consumers would like to buy locally grown, organic produce, naturally fertilized and free from chemical sprays and pesticides. More and more farmstands are answering their needs.

The vegetable's growing season will always be an integral part of the farmstand even though in our time there is no longer a particular season for a particular vegetable or fruit. The east coast is deluged with west coast asparagus and giant strawberries in late winter. Their flavor may not be up to expectation and the price outrageous, but asparagus lovers will buy asparagus, no matter what the price. This is almost a sacrilege to some purists who believe that every season is signaled by the produce it produces. For those who lived in the period of time when you could tell the season by the appearance of a certain vegetable in the market, all this availability is not necessarily a welcome development. But this is the new time and even though there are some who wait for the vegetable-appropriate season we can't help but give in to the current trend that allows us to have freshness all year round.

The farmstand's season has been expanded to allow for more produce, more income, and very importantly, more farmers enjoying the fruits of their labors for a longer period of time. What we are seeing is nature's bounty at its glory and a modern day "gold rush" for the American farmer.

At a busy local farmstand in Woodbury, New York, Terry Meyer, the proprietress, gave a delightful description of her family's business. "Our farm has been here since the 1920s but the stand was developed in the 1950s. In the 1920s to 1940s everyone had a backyard garden around here. They didn't need to buy vegetables from someone else. Now, they all want the perfect lawn and manicured beds. I hear women tell their husbands, when they want to buy vegetable or herb plants, 'I don't want those things in my yard.'" In the spring, she sells flower plants. As their farm fresh, home grown vegetables come in, the flower greenhouse closes and the vegetable stand opens.

Variety is "in" and many farms have added endive and mini veggies to their roster of produce. Tiny corn, patti-pan squash, baby zucchini, baby bok choy, and mini carrots are offered on a regular basis at farmstands and greenmarkets. Purple broccoli and cauliflower, white eggplant and other new varieties of old favorites appear at some of the stands although the search still goes on for the sweetest and most tender ear of corn.

Sang Lee Farms, located in Peconic, New York, has been a purveyor of specialty and Asian greens for over fifty years. The original farm was started by Fred Lee's father and uncles and was located in Huntington, Long Island. A move in 1964 to the East Moriches area was followed by a move to Peconic in 1987 where they now farm two-hundred-ninety acres. With the Long Island wine country as a backdrop the Lees are growing snow pea shoots, asparagus and cilantro, and their specialties include baby spinach, baby arugula, baby kale, and baby romaine. These are popular items with the local chefs who snip or cut the items as desired. Mesclun is a big seller and combines fourteen different types of greens including tatsol, snow pea shoots, and tung ho. Each leaf is harvested by hand and added to the mix. Sang Lee Farms' mesclun is sold with snippets of fresh flower petals. To quote their newsletter, "Our mesclun is Fresh-lee-cut every day, sometimes twice-a-day." Packages of "Fresh-lee-cut" mesclun can also be purchased by mail order. (see page 2) The Lees have been featured on the *Martha Stewart Show* with their Asian Cole Slaw recipe.

"Where have all the farmstands gone?" Fortunately the answer to that question is that they are alive and well and thriving all over the United States. There are alternate terms for the farmstand like farmers' market, greenmarket, or greengrocer, but the essence or the thought is the same—a place to buy the freshest, tastiest, and most beautiful of produce; and an opportunity to mingle and to exchange recipes and ideas and feel that it is time well spent.

Footnotes

1-Schieber and Vatter and Faulkner. *American Economic History*. Harper & Row, 1976, pp. 138-9.
2-Sloan, Eric. *America Yesterday*, Funk & Wagnalls, 1956.

FARMSTAND RULES
Vegetable Know-How

While the art of baking requires exact measurement, the art of cooking with vegetables needs not be quite so exact and you can take some license with your ingredient measurements. A specified cup of chopped carrots may leave you with a pitifully small extra piece of carrot that you are loathe to throw away and may not be in the mood to eat. What to do? Use it! That tiny piece will not throw your recipe off. With this in mind we would like to make life a bit easier and shopping more fun. We offer you this rule of thumb measurement chart:

Farmer's Rule of Thumb Measurement

This guide will provide the farmstand shopper with criteria for approximate measuring without measuring equipment. While it is called "rule of thumb" it is really "measurement by eye."

asparagus:	5 to 6—1 portion
carrots:	2 medium—1 cup cut into medium dices
corn:	1 large ear—1 cup of kernels
garlic:	1 large clove—1 teaspoon, minced, 3/4 teaspoon, crushed
fruit:	baseball size—1 cup, diced
lemon:	grated zest of 1 lemon—approximately 1 teaspoon
lettuce:	4 leaves—1 cup, shredded
mesclun:	1 average sized handful—1 cup portion
mushroom caps:	7 or 8 small—1 cup, sliced
onion:	1 medium—1 cup, chopped
pepper:	1 very large—1 cup cut into medium dices
tomato:	1 baseball size—1 cup, diced
zucchini:	1 small—1 cup grated or diced
lemon:	1 squeezed—approximately 1/4 cup of juice

Picking the Pick of the Crop

Know your vegetables! If they don t look fresh don't buy them unless they are essential to your recipe. Colors should be bright. The items should be free from blemishes and the skin should be smooth. Purchase your perishables in amounts you can use within two or three days and store them in specially made plastic bags, the kind with tiny holes. Keep them in the vegetable drawer of your refrigerator. Keep potatoes, winter squash, turnips, onions, and garlic in a cool place. Refrigeration is not necessary for these winter vegetables.

Artichokes: Look for tightly closed globes. Pick the ones with the least bruising.
Asparagus: Look for firm, closed tops. Be sure the stems are not dry and shriveled.
Broccoli: Yellow spots mean the broccoli is old—look for solid green.
Cabbage: Tightly packed leaves for cole slaw. Loosely packed leaves to stuff.
Cauliflower: Blemishes indicate greater age. The heads should be pure white.
Corn: Strip the corn husks to expose about 3 inches of the top. Kernels should be firm and tight and not bruised.
Cucumber: Avoid any with soft spots and shriveled areas.
Eggplant: Smooth, shiny skin and firmness are the key to good eggplant. Old eggplants are very seedy and those seeds can contribute to bitterness.
Endive: Check that the tips are not brown and leaves are tightly closed.
Garlic: When held in the hand a head of garlic should feel solid with no air spots to indicate older garlic. Sprouts are bitter and need to be cut away.
Mushrooms, white domestic: Caps should be tightly closed with a creamy white coloring and no bruises.
Onions: Avoid those with soft spots and sprouting.
Peppers: Skin should be shiny without bruised and soft areas.
Potatoes: Watch out for sprouts (eyes) and avoid any that are soft and bruised.
String beans: String beans should be firm, free of brown spots, and bright green.
Zucchini: Skin should be shiny and smooth.

VEGETABLE COOKERY METHODS

Blanch: Uncooked vegetables are put into boiling water and removed as soon as the water returns to a rolling boil. They are then plunged into ice water to stop further cooking. To freeze many vegetables such as green beans or corn, blanch them first. Blanching also sets the vegetables color that can be used *al dente* in salads.

Boil: A moist heat cookery method; vegetables are cooked in boiling (212° F.) water or stock. The boiling bubbles break the surface of the water vigorously.

Braise: This term is used more frequently with meat cookery. It indicates lightly sautéing a vegetable, adding a small amount of liquid, then covering the pan and simmering until done. When cooking red cabbage or kale or collards, the dish may be braised.

Broil: A dry-heat method where the heat source usually emanates from above the food. The vegetable is cooked on a rack by direct heat as in broiled tomato slices.

Frying: (cooking in 1-inch or less of any type of fat)
Deep Frying: A vegetable is cooked in several inches of fat with the temperature carefully maintained at 350° F. All fat has a combustion point and will burst into flames if it reaches a greater temperature. Breaded okra, French fried potatoes, fritters, and croquettes are deep fried. Thermostatically controlled electric deep-fat fryers are best for keeping the fat temperature in a safe range that also cooks evenly.

Stir-Frying: A small amount of fat, usually oil, in a slope-sided deep pan, is heated, vegetables added, and stirred constantly with cooking chopsticks or a wooden spoon, until the vegetables are lightly coated with oil, crisp cooked, and then frequently flavored with a light sauce. These vegetables maintain bright color and *al dente* (slightly crisp) texture.

Grill: This is a dry-heat method with the heat source coming either from above or below the food. Ridged grill pans for use on top of the stove do a good job on vegetables that have been brushed with olive oil and seasoned with salt, pepper, and fresh or dried herbs. On outdoor grills, the same method applies. For smaller pieces there are special fine-screen holders to lay over the larger grill rack.

Par-boil: The "par" means partial. Vegetables are partially cooked by boiling first, then completed by a second method. If vegetables such as potatoes and carrots are to be roasted along with a meat, they cook faster if par-boiled until half done and then added to the roasting pan.

Poach: To cook a vegetable slowly in a liquid kept just below the boiling point.

Pressure Cook: Vegetables are cooked in a small amount of liquid under pressure so they cook more quickly. It's a satisfactory method for vegetables such as beets and legumes that are long cooking. Follow the instructions that come with your pressure cooker to operate it safely.

Roast: We usually associate roasting with meats. However, many vegetables are now being roasted in an oven, often wrapped in foil with various flavorings included. Roasting, like baking, is a dry-heat method.

Sauté: This is a very common term that means cooking quickly and lightly in a small amount of fat or oil. Vegetables may be partially cooked this way, then added to another dish or cooked completely, as with a rapeed (shredded) zucchini.

Simmer: To cook slowly in a liquid kept under the boiling temperature. There should be tiny little bubbles in the cooking liquid.

Steam: This method of cooking vegetables helps retain the most nutrients. It is a moist-heat cookery method. Vegetables are placed in a container such as a strainer or special steamer basket and placed over boiling water which doesn't touch the bottom of the steamer basket. A cover is placed over the basket and the heat reduced just enough to keep the water boiling. The steam that is produced cooks the vegetables.

Sweat: To sweat a vegetable, it is placed in a pan with a small amount of fat or oil. A round of parchment or waxed paper is cut to fit the pan size and is laid directly on the food pieces, then covered. The heat is kept very low and the vegetable "sweats" under the paper and cooks lightly.

FRIED ARTICHOKES

(1) Fill a large bowl with cold water and add the lemon juice. Set aside.

(2) Cut the stem from the bottom of each artichoke. Slice around the bottom to create a smooth surface. Remove the coarse outer leaves until you reach the tender yellow leaves.

NOTE: *The outer leaves can be steamed and served with melted butter. They will keep, refrigerated, cooked or uncooked, about 1 week.*

(3) Slice the artichoke vertically into 1-inch to 1 1/2-inch slices. With a small paring knife remove any purple spiky fuzz. Add the slices to the lemon water. Repeat with each artichoke.

(4) Bring a 2-quart pot of water to a boil, add 2 teaspoons of salt and the artichokes. Simmer for about 10 minutes or until the hearts are barely tender. Drain. (These can be refrigerated for up to two days before frying.)

(5) For the batter, combine the eggs, cheese, parsley, salt and pepper in a shallow bowl. Pour the flour into a similar bowl.

(6) Heat 1/4 cup of oil or enough to form a 1/4-inch layer in a fry pan.

(7) Dip a few artichoke slices into the flour, coat well, dip into the eggs, coat well, re-dip into the flour. Fry in the oil until golden on both sides.

NOTE: *Drain on paper towel. Repeat with the remaining slices. Serve as soon as possible for the best flavor. They can be reheated or served at room temperature.*

NOTE: *The task of preparing artichokes may seem daunting but it is worth your while to make them a part of your recipe repertoire. Their subtle flavor is unsurpassed and in this particular recipe they are wonderful foils for the bite of Pecorino cheese. Here much of the nitty-gritty work can be done one or two days in advance. For best flavor, fry just before serving.*

 INGREDIENTS

juice of 2 lemons
4 large artichokes
2 teaspoons of salt

BATTER
3 eggs, lightly beaten
1 cup of grated Pecorino cheese
1/4 cup of chopped flat leaf
   parsley
salt and pepper to taste
2 cups of flour
1/2 to 1 cup of Mazola corn oil
   for frying

SERVES 4-6

BABY ARTICHOKES
AND PARMESAN SALAD

(1) Pull outer leaves from the artichokes down to the center tender leaves. Slice off 1 1/2 inches from the top, spread the leaves open and with a paring knife or your fingers remove any prickly, purple center.

(2) Pare around the base to remove stem and expose tender heart.

(3) Add the artichoke hearts to the bowl of lemon-water. Keep chilled for 1 to 24 hours.

(4) When ready to serve: Arrange the greens on 4 individual salad plates.

(5) Drain the artichokes. Using the largest slicing side of a 4 sided grater, a mandoline or a very sharp knife, thinly slice the artichokes and divide over the arugula.

(6) Using the same grater side, shave the Parmesan onto the salad and sprinkle on the walnuts. The Parmesan can be shaved in advance and set aside, covered.

(7) Drizzle each with some olive oil and Balsamic vinegar. Season with salt and pepper to taste.

 INGREDIENTS

1 pound of baby artichokes
juice of 2 lemons squeezed into a medium bowl of cold water
1 large bunch of arugula or 4 handfuls of mesclun, rinsed and dried
1/3 pound of good Parmesan cheese
1/2 cup of coarsely chopped walnuts (optional)
1/3 to 1/2 cup of extra-virgin olive oil
1/8 to 1/4 cup of balsamic vinegar
salt and pepper to taste

NOTE: This is a very European way to serve those tiny baby artichokes when they are in season. They lend themselves so well to this delicate dish. As always, quality is important and a very good Parmesan cheese is essential. This elegant salad can be served as an appetizer or salad course.

SERVES 4

ARTICHOKES
STUFFED 'N STEAMED

(1) To prepare the artichokes, cut off any stem including bottom row of leaves. Snip sharp points off tips of all leaves with a kitchen shears. Using the three middle fingers of both hands, gently spread open the rows of leaves so the artichoke looks like a flower opening. Wash artichoke well and drain upside down on paper toweling.

(2) Blend together the bread crumbs, cheese, and all seasonings except oil.

(3) Use a teaspoon to sprinkle the crumb mixture over the artichokes, directing it evenly between the rows of leaves. Tap the artichoke on your work surface occasionally so the crumbs settle to the bottom of the rows.

(4) Drizzle 1 teaspoon of the olive oil over each artichoke. Set them in a steamer basket over boiling water, cover, reduce the heat but keep water steaming and steam for 25 minutes or more until a lower leaf can be pulled out easily.

(5) To serve, set the artichokes on a plate and pick off 1 leaf at a time. (See note)

INGREDIENTS

2 large artichokes
2 tablespoons of bread crumbs
2 tablespoons of grated Parmesan or Romano cheese
2 tablespoons of freshly chopped parsley
1 tablespoon of freshly chopped basil or 1 1/2 teaspoons dried
1/2 teaspoon of dried oregano
1/4 teaspoon of salt
2 cloves of garlic, minced
2 teaspoons of olive oil for drizzling

NOTE: To eat them, scrape off the crumb filling at the base of each leaf with your teeth. Have a dish ready for finished leaves. Keep eating this way until you reach the heart. Remove any of the fibrous choke; sprinkle the heart with salt and pepper and enjoy your reward -the tender, delicious artichoke heart.

SERVES 2-4, SHARED

ASPARAGUS RISOTTO
WITH CHRISTINE'S FRESH BASIL OIL

(1) Bring the stock to a boil and reduce to a simmer. Keep at a simmer during the entire cooking process.

(2) In a large saucepan, heat the olive oil and add the onion. Cover and allow to sweat for 2 to 3 minutes or until onions are transparent.

(3) Add the carrots, asparagus, zucchini, peas, and 1 cup of stock. Cook, covered, on medium heat for 5 minutes.

(4) Add 4 tablespoons of basil olive oil and the rice. Combine well to coat the rice.

(5) Add a cup of simmering stock to the rice and stir often to prevent sticking.

(6) As the stock is absorbed, continue to add the stock in one cup increments, being sure that after each addition the liquid is allowed to evaporate.

(7) Cook until rice mixture is creamy but the kernels have a firm center, approximately 18 to 20 minutes.

(7) Remove from heat. Season with salt and pepper to taste and stir in the butter.

(8) Drizzle some of the basil olive oil, in a swirl pattern, onto the bottom of four soup bowls. Portion out the risotto among the bowls. Sprinkle with the Parmesan and garnish with some fresh basil leaves. Finish with a last decorative drizzle of basil olive oil over the rice. Serve immediately.

INGREDIENTS

10 cups of chicken or vegetable
    stock
1 medium onion, cut into
    1-inch dices
2 tablespoons of olive oil
1 cup of 1/2-inch diced carrots
1 cup of 1/2-inch diced asparagus
1 cup of 1/2-inch diced zucchini
1 cup of fresh peas
4 tablespoons of basil oil
3 cups of arborio rice *
Parmesan cheese to taste,
    shaved or grated
7 or 8 fresh basil leaves
salt and pepper to taste
3 tablespoons of unsalted butter
basil oil for garnish (see page 35)

SERVES 6 AS A MAIN DISH
OR 8 AS A SIDE DISH

*While you can use regular rice, the
authentic texture and creaminess is only
achieved with the use of arborio rice,
available in specialty food markets.*

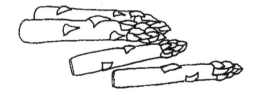

33

ASPARAGUS MUSHROOM PUFF

(1) Line a baking pan, large enough to hold a 9 or 10-inch pie pan, with a layer of foil.

Preheat the oven to 350° F.

(2) Pour the corn oil into the pie pan and place the pan on the lined baking pan. Heat in the oven for 10 minutes.

(3) While the oil is heating, combine the flour, milk, eggs, sage, salt, and pepper.

(4) Lightly brush the asparagus with some of the olive oil and toss the mushrooms with the remaining olive oil.

(5) Remove the pan from the oven and raise the heat to 375° F.

(6) Pour the batter into the heated oil. Place the asparagus on top of the batter in spoke like fashion with the tips at the outer edge. Sprinkle on the mushrooms and extra salt and pepper.

(8) Bake for 30 to 40 minutes or until batter is golden and puffed.

(9) When golden and puffed, place the oiled basil leaves decoratively on top and bake 5 more minutes.

INGREDIENTS

1/8 cup of Mazola corn oil
1 cup of flour
1 1/2 cups of milk
2 eggs
1 tablespoon of fresh sage leaves, minced
1 teaspoon of salt
1 teaspoon of pepper
1/8 to 1/4 cup of olive oil
1/2 pound of fresh asparagus, trimmed to about 4 inches long
1 cup of sliced mushrooms
fresh basil leaves lightly coated with olive oil
salt and pepper to taste

NOTE: Serve warm as a main luncheon course with a salad and a dry white wine or use as a side dish for roasts or poultry.

SERVES 4 AS A MAIN COURSE 6 TO 8 AS A SIDE

CHRISTINE'S FRESH BASIL OIL

(1) Combine the basil leaves and olive oil in a blender. Pour into the plastic bottle and store in the refrigerator for up to two weeks. Remove from the fridge about 1 hour before using and shake well.

NOTE: *This mixture can also be thinned with extra olive oil, seasoned with salt and pepper, and used to brush over baked chicken or fish.*

 INGREDIENTS

1/2 cup of fresh basil leaves, rinsed and dried
1/4 cup + 2 tablespoons of olive oil
1 plastic bottle with a thin nozzle top

BASIL PINEAPPLE COOLER

(1) In a blender, combine the pineapple juice and basil leaves for 15 seconds or until the mix resembles a milkshake.
(2) Pour over ice in a wine glass. Add sparkling water and/or wine to taste or serve as is.
(3) Garnish with a carrot stick and minced basil.

 INGREDIENTS

2 cups of cold pineapple juice
12 large basil leaves, rinsed
sparkling water or white wine (optional)
slim carrot strips
minced basil

NOTE: *A drizzle of fresh basil oil as a garnish can turn a plain dish into a masterpiece. Basil is sometimes sold with the roots still attached and holds well in a glass of cold water or wrapped in paper toweling and kept in the fridge.*

STRING BEANS
WITH FRESH HERBS

(1) Add the beans to enough lightly salted boiling water to cover. Cook until just tender, about 10 minutes.

(2) While beans cook, melt butter over low heat, but do not brown. Add the celery, onion, parsley, basil, rosemary, and garlic. Let simmer together gently for 5 minutes.

(3) When beans are done, drain (saving liquid to use as vegetable stock), and place into a warm serving dish. Pour the butter–herb mixture over the top and stir gently to combine ingredients.

NOTE: *A most savory way to serve garden fresh beans with freshly picked herbs.*

INGREDIENTS

1 pound of fresh green beans, washed, ends removed, and cut into 1-inch pieces on the diagonal

1/4 cup of butter

1/2 cup of finely diced celery

1/2 cup of finely diced onion

2 tablespoons of chopped parsley

2 teaspoons of finely shredded fresh basil

1 teaspoon of chopped fresh rosemary

1 clove of garlic, minced or put through a garlic press

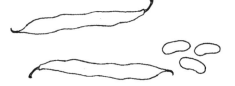

SERVES 4

STRING BEANS

(1) Cook beans in a generous amount of boiling, salted water until crisp tender, about 10 minutes. Drain, saving the cooking liquid. Keep warm.

(2) While beans cook, crisp fry the bacon. Remove from pan, drain on a paper towel and crumble. Drain off all but a small amount of the bacon drippings and add the tablespoon of butter to the pan.

(3) Lightly sauté the diced onion in the butter. In a small bowl, combine the vinegar, water, sugar, and cornstarch thoroughly. Remove the pan with the onion and butter from the heat and whisk in the vinegar mixture. Return to heat and let mixture bubble and thicken, adding some of the bean cooking liquid if sauce gets too thick.

(4) To serve, place hot beans into a warmed serving bowl, add the crumbled bacon to the sauce and pour over the beans.

 INGREDIENTS

1 pound of very fresh, unblemished string beans, washed, ends trimmed, and cut at an angle into 1/2 to 1-inch pieces
3 slices of bacon
1 tablespoon of butter
1 small onion, finely diced
1/2 cup of cider vinegar
1/4 cup of water
1/2 cup of sugar
1 tablespoon+ 1 teaspoon of cornstarch

NOTE: This is fourth a generation recipe.

SERVES 4

CRIMSON BEETS
FRESH BEETS COATED WITH A CLEAR SWEET-SOUR SAUCE

(1) Remove beet green tops*, leaving about a 1 inch stem on the beets. Wash beets well. Cover with water in a 2-quart pot, bring to a boil, cover, reduce heat and boil gently until beets are tender (about 30 minutes or more).

(2) Remove beets from the water, let cool and slip off the skins and remaining stems. Cut into 1/2-inch dice or, if the beets are small, you may slice them about 1/8-inch thick. Set aside while you make the sauce.

(3) Melt the butter slowly in a sauté pan or medium skillet. Whisk the remaining ingredients together in a bowl, then whisk into melted butter. Stir until sauce becomes thickened and clear. If too thick, add a little bit of the beet cooking liquid.

(4) Add the diced beets to the sauce and gently blend together with a wooden spoon. Heat thoroughly before serving.

* **Beet Greens**: Prepare like spinach and serve with a dot of butter.

 INGREDIENTS

1 bunch of beets—about 4 medium
1 tablespoon of butter
1 tablespoon of cornstarch
1/4 cup + 1 tablespoon of cider vinegar
1/4 cup of sugar
1/4 cup of cooking liquid from beets
1 teaspoon of onion juice and pulp**
1/2 teaspoon of salt
1/8 teaspoon of white pepper

**If you grate onion on the fine side of a 4-sided grater, only the juice comes through with some very fine pulp on the front.*

SERVES 4

BROCCOLI AND CAULIFLOWER
STIR FRY

(1) Heat a large, heavy skillet or wok. Add 2 tablespoons of the oil and rotate the pan to coat well.
(2) Allow the oil to smoke for a few seconds. Add the broccoli and 1/4 cup of water; cover, and allow to cook over medium heat for 5-7 minutes. Broccoli's color should remain an intense green.
(3) With a slotted spoon, transfer to a large bowl.
(4) Add and heat 2 tablespoons of the remaining oil, allow to smoke and then add the cauliflower and 1/4 cup of water. Cover and allow to cook over medium heat for 7 minutes. Add to the broccoli.
(5) Add the remaining oil, heat and add the red pepper, ginger, and garlic. Combine well and stir fry on high heat for about 5 minutes or until any liquid has evaporated.
(6) Return the broccoli and cauliflower to the pan and add the soy sauce, sesame oil, and walnuts. Combine well being sure to pick the sauce from the bottom of the pan to coat the veggies. Stir fry 2 more minutes. The veggies should be tenderly crisp.

 INGREDIENTS

2 cups of broccoli flowerets, rinsed (stems may be peeled and used in this recipe)
2 cups of cauliflower flowerets, rinsed (cauliflower is short-stemmed—use it all)
1 cup of diced red pepper
1/3 cup of corn oil
1 tablespoon of grated fresh ginger
2 gloves of garlic, minced
2 tablespoons of soy sauce
2 teaspoons of sesame oil
1/2 cup of walnut pieces (optional)

SERVES 4-6

CREAM OF BROCCOLI SOUP

(1) Melt the butter or margarine in a 2 or 3 quart saucepan. Add the onion or shallot and saute lightly.

(2) With a whisk, blend in the flour. Over medium heat, stir and cook for a couple of minutes. Remove the pan from the heat and whisk in the milk and the broth. Return pan to heat. Stir and cook on medium until mixture bubbles and thickens. Set aside.

(3) In a food processor, puree the broccoli. Add some of the hot sauce to the bowl and process another 30 to 60 seconds. Pour back into the saucepan, stir and taste. If you want added flavor, crumble in half of the Knorr bouillon cube which is salty, stir to dissolve and taste again. Add more, if needed, along with pepper to taste.

(4) Simmer a few minutes to develop flavor. Should you want the soup thicker, you can add 2 tablespoons of instant mashed potatoes, then stir and simmer a few more minutes. Add croutons or a dollop of sour cream for a finishing touch.

NOTE: Nutmeg goes well with all the above mentioned vegetables. Curry powder (1/2 teaspoon) goes particularly well with squash. While teaching a class on stocks, Francois Dionet of l'Academie de Cuisine in Maryland said, "When I have lots of stock in my freezer I feel really rich. I know I have the basis for many different dishes and sauces."

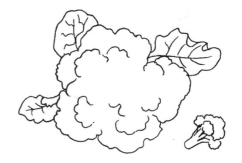

NOTE: *Tempted by the beautiful displays of fresh vegetables at your farm-stand, you may buy and cook more than you can eat at one meal. What do you do with 1 - 1 1/2 cups of leftover cooked veggies? With home-made chicken or vegetable stock on hand or even canned broth or bouillon cubes and some seasonings, these leftovers become tasty soups for lunch or a first course for dinner, within minutes. This recipe calls for broccoli, but asparagus, spinach, squash, or cauliflower can be used just as deliciously. In December, 1999, a newspaper recap article of the past century noted that broccoli was introduced to the United States from Italy in 1928.*

 INGREDIENTS

2 tablespoons of butter or margarine
1 small onion or a large shallot, finely diced
2 tablespoons of flour
1 cup each of low-fat milk and chicken broth
1 1/2 cups of leftover cooked broccoli
 salt and pepper to taste
1/8-1/4 teaspoon of freshly grated nutmeg
1/2 of a Knorr chicken bouillon cube, if needed for flavor
instant mashed potatoes for added thickening, if desired
Fresh croutons and/or sour cream or plain yogurt for garnish (optional)

SERVES 3-4

BRUSSELS SPROUTS
WITH CHESTNUTS

(1) Bring 2 quarts of water to a boil; add the sprouts and baking soda. Simmer gently for about 20 minutes or until sprouts are barely tender when pierced with a fork.

(2) When done, drain, transfer to a bowl and set aside.

(3) In a sauté pan cook the bacon or pancetta until quite crisp. Drain off some of the fat and add the onion. Sauté 5 minutes, combining well.

(4) Add the chestnuts, sauté 5 minutes.

(5) Add the Brussels sprouts, combine and sauté to heat through, about another 5 minutes.

(6) Season with salt and pepper and serve.

* *Baking soda maintains the deep green color of the Brussels sprouts.*

NOTE: *If you stop at a country farmstand in early fall you should find long, thick, green stalks of Brussels sprouts. At first you might not realize that you are*

 INGREDIENTS

1 pound of Brussels sprouts, rinsed
1 teaspoon of baking soda*
3 slices of bacon or pancetta, diced
1 cup of minced onion
1 cup of boiled or roasted, peeled chestnuts (Unsweetened, canned chestnuts may be used)
salt and pepper to taste

looking at Brussels sprouts as the stalks look like small trees. The little cabbage heads are attached to the stalk and must be snapped off to cook. Try to find even-sized little heads so they cook evenly. If you buy an extra stalk you can use it as a seasonal centerpiece surrounded by colorful gourds and pumpkins.

SERVES 4

BRUSSELS SPROUTS NIBBLERS

(1) Trim the base off each Brussels sprout and remove any loose or blemished outer leaves. Rinse in fresh water. Bring 3 cups of water to a boil in a 2-quart pan, then add 1 teaspoon of salt. Add the Brussels sprouts and boil gently for 6 to 8 minutes. They should be bright green and barely tender.

(2) Remove the sprouts from the pan with a slotted spoon and plunge them into ice water to cool quickly. After about 1 minute, drain and transfer the sprouts to a glass bowl.

(3) Measure vinegar, garlic, mustard, and pepper into the bowl of a small food processor or blender. Cover and blend until smooth. Slowly add the olive oil and blend just until well mixed and slightly opaque.

(4) Pour the dressing over the cooled vegetable and turn several times to coat each head. Large heads may be cut in half to allow the marinade flavors to penetrate. Cover with plastic wrap and leave at room temperature for serving the same day. Refrigerate if serving the next day. Stir gently before serving, to coat each head well. Serve with frilly toothpicks.

 INGREDIENTS

1 pound of Brussels sprouts
1 teaspoon of salt
3 tablespoons of seasoned rice vinegar (available in Oriental food shops as well as supermarkets)
2 cloves of garlic, peeled and minced
1 teaspoon of stone-ground mustard
1/4 teaspoon of freshly ground black pepper
1/4 cup of extra-virgin olive oil

NOTE: *Do not overcook them; as Julia Child says in* Mastering the Art of French Cooking, *"Brussels sprouts should be bright green, fresh-tasting and have the slightest suggestion of crunch at the core."*

SERVES 4-6

ZESTY CABBAGE AND TOMATOES
WITH CARAWAY SEEDS

(1) Combine tomatoes, cabbage, and water in a saucepan and bring to a boil. Reduce heat and simmer about 10 minutes, uncovered.

(2) Add salt, pepper, and caraway seeds. Simmer another 10 minutes.

(3) Put butter and flour in a custard cup and heat on low in microwave until butter is melted. Blend butter and flour until smooth.

(4) Stir into cabbage mixture and simmer another 5 minutes to thicken the liquid and blend the flavors.

(5) Serve with a generous topping of chopped fresh chives or parsley.

INGREDIENTS

4 medium tomatoes, peeled*
    and cut into 1/2-inch dices
4 cups of coarsely shredded
    green cabbage
1 cup of water
1 teaspoon of salt
1/2 teaspoon of freshly ground
    black pepper
2 teaspoons of caraway seeds,
    lightly toasted
1 tablespoon of unsalted butter
1 tablespoon of flour
chopped chives or parsley for
    garnish

To peel tomatoes, plunge into boiling water for 1 minute. Remove to a bowl of cold water, slit the skin, and it will slip off easily.

SERVES 6

RED CABBAGE SALAD

(1) Combine cabbage, lettuce, cucumber, tomatoes, radishes, and scallions in a large salad bowl.
(2) Whisk oil, lemon juice, oregano, honey, and cumin together and toss with vegetables.
(3) Cover and marinate for 3 to 4 hours in the refrigerator.
(4) Just before serving, mix the cumin and salt together and sprinkle over the salad mix. Serve.

INGREDIENTS

3 cups of shredded red cabbage
1/2 head of romaine lettuce, shredded
1 cucumber, diced
2 tomatoes, diced
6 radishes, diced
4 scallions, cut into 1/2-inch pieces

Dressing

1/4 cup of vegetable oil
1/4 cup + 2 tablespoons of fresh lemon juice
1/4 teaspoon of dried oregano
1 tablespoon of honey
1/4 teaspoon of ground cumin

Add just before serving

3/4 teaspoon of cumin
1 teaspoon of salt

SERVES 6

CURRIED SWEET CARROTS

(1) Melt the butter in a large sauté pan.

(2) Add the carrots and the water or stock. Cover. Simmer over medium-low heat until tender, about 15 minutes.

(3) Remove cover and simmer allowing any liquid to evaporate.

(4) Stir in the brown sugar and curry powder. Combine well and cook uncovered until mixture is slightly syrupy and you can smell the curry powder.

(5) Transfer to a serving bowl and sprinkle with parsley.

NOTE: There is no need to boil carrots and have all their nutritive value thrown out with the boiling water. Just a small amount of liquid over a medium-low heat will cook your carrots and all the nutrients will be passed on to you along with their wonderful sweet flavor.

 INGREDIENTS

2 tablespoons of butter

1 pound of carrots, sliced 1/2-inch thick on the diagonal

1/2 cup of water or light chicken or vegetable stock

2 tablespoons of brown sugar

1/2 to 2 teaspoons of curry powder to taste

1/4 cup of minced flat leaf parsley

SERVES 4

CAULIFLOWER WITH HERBED
BUTTERED CRUMBS

(1) Remove the leaves from the cauliflower and wash it well.

(2) Bring a pot of water to a boil, deep and large enough to hold the whole head of cauliflower. When the water boils, add the salt and cauliflower, top down. Boil gently five minutes, covered, and carefully turn so the top of the head is up. Boil 3 minutes longer. The whole head should be tender. Remove carefully to a colander to drain.

(3) While the cauliflower cooks, melt the butter over medium heat in a small skillet. When butter bubbles, add the snipped herbs; stir, then add the bread crumbs. Stir gently until the crumbs are nicely browned.

(4) Place the drained cauliflower on a large plate. Surround with parsley and thyme sprigs. Spoon the buttered crumbs over the top. Use a large spoon to cut serving sizes from the head, making sure every portion receives some of the buttered crumbs.

 INGREDIENTS

1 medium-sized head of farm fresh, snowy white cauliflower, 1 1/2-2 pounds

1 tablespoon of salt for the cooking water

2 tablespoons of salted butter

1/4 cup of unseasoned bread crumbs

1 tablespoon of freshly snipped herbs, such as thyme or basil and a little rosemary

NOTE: *Sometimes the simpler a vegetable is prepared, the better it tastes.*

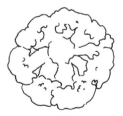

SERVES 4-6

GIANT SWISS CHARD POCKET

DOUGH

 INGREDIENTS

1 package of Rapid Rise yeast
1/2 teaspoon of sugar
1 cup of warm water (not more than 110° F.)
1 teaspoon of olive oil
2 1/2 - 2 3/4 cups of all-purpose flour
1 teaspoon of salt

(1) Stir together the yeast, sugar, and water in a glass measuring cup. Let stand a few minutes until it starts to foam. Stir in the olive oil.
(2) Stir 2 1/4 cups of the flour and salt together in a medium-sized glass bowl. Add yeast mixture and stir until a dough forms. Pour 1/4 cup of flour onto a work surface, scrape the dough onto the flour and knead dough, gently at first, for about 5 minutes, flouring your hands and the work surface if the dough becomes sticky. (You may not use a full 2 3/4 cup of flour.)
(3) Wash and dry the bowl you mixed the dough in, then oil it lightly. Place the dough in the bowl, turning to coat the surface with oil. Cover with plastic wrap. Put a cup of hot water in the microwave. Place the dough bowl next to it. Microwave on the lowest setting (100 degrees) for 10 minutes. Rotate bowl and microwave another 5 minutes at lowest setting. The dough should be almost doubled in bulk but let it remain in a warm place until it has doubled. Alternatively, instead of the microwave, let rise in a warm place for about an hour.

To Make the Filling;

(1) Roughly chop the Swiss chard and steam cook, covered, with a minimum amount of water, for 5 minutes. Drain, pressing out any excess liquid, and set aside.

(2) In a large skillet, heat the olive oil and lightly sauté the garlic and onion. Add the drained Swiss chard, salami or ham, olives, pignoli nuts, capers, and cheese. Taste and add salt and freshly ground pepper to taste. Remove from heat.

Preheat the oven to 375° F.

(3) Press out the dough in a lightly oiled 14 or 16-inch pizza pan. The dough should be quite thin with thicker edges. Place the filling over half the dough. Fold the other half over the filling, sealing the edges. You now have a large turnover. Brush with olive oil, pierce several times with a fork and bake in a 375° F. oven for about 35 minutes or until golden brown.

INGREDIENTS

1 pound of frozen pizza dough or use the included dough recipe

1 pound of Swiss chard or escarole or a combination of both, washed, and roughly chopped

2 tablespoons of olive oil + 1 tablespoon for brushing dough before baking

1 clove of garlic, minced

1 medium red onion, finely chopped

1 ounce of ham, pepperoni, or salami, cut into small pieces (2 tablespoons)

2 tablespoons of oil cured olives, pitted and chopped

2 tablespoons of pignoli nuts, toasted

1 tablespoon of small capers

1 ounce (2 tablespoons) of finely shaved provolone or Parmesan cheese pieces

salt and pepper to taste

SERVES 4

SWISS CHARD
WITH FRESH TOMATOES AND PENNE

(1) You should have about 3 cups of leaves and 2 to 3 cups of stems.

(2) In a large saucepan, heat 1 tablespoon of the oil. Add the garlic and onion. Sauté 2 minutes.

(3) Add the stems, stir and cover. Simmer 5 to 7 minutes or until stems are just tender.

(4) Add the chard leaves, combine and simmer 5 minutes, covered.

(5) Push the chard to the sides of the pan, allow any liquid to simmer off. Add the remaining tablespoon of oil. Allow to heat and then add the tomatoes to the center. Simmer on medium-high, uncovered, about 3 to 5 minutes.

(6) Combine the chard and tomatoes. Add salt and pepper to taste and sauté, uncovered for 7 to 10 minutes.

(7) Stir in the cooked penne.

(8) Season with salt and pepper and serve with meat, fish, or poultry or as part of a vegetarian meal.

 INGREDIENTS

1 large bunch of Swiss chard, rinsed, stems cut into 2-inch pieces, leaves coarsely chopped

1 cup of fresh, peeled, seeded, and chopped ripe tomatoes (or canned whole tomatoes, drained)

2 tablespoons of olive oil

2 cloves of garlic, minced

1/3 cup of onion, minced

salt and pepper to taste

3/4 of a pound of penne, cooked and drained

NOTE: *Swiss chard may be related to the beet family and was cultivated in prehistoric times. Often referred to as chard it has nothing to do with Switzerland. From the The World Encyclopedia of Food by L. Patrick Coyle Jr., Facts on File, New York, 1982.*

SERVES 4

ANNIKA'S WILTED COLLARDS
(KALE OR MUSTARD GREENS)

(1) After washing greens, stack them together with all the stems facing in the same direction. Slice across the stack into 1-inch pieces.

(2) In a deep pot that has a lid, heat the olive oil. Sauté the onion and shallots until golden, about 10 minutes.

(3) Stir in the stock and garlic. Place the prepared greens on top. Sprinkle with salt and pepper, cover the pan and cook about 20 minutes. Turn the greens several times during the cooking period.

(4) Sprinkle on the lemon juice. Toss and serve warm with a little extra olive oil, lemon wedges, and grated egg.

INGREDIENTS

2 tablespoons of mild olive oil
1 medium onion, chopped
2 shallots, chopped
1/4 cup of chicken or vegetable stock
2 small garlic cloves, minced
1 1/2-2 pounds of fresh collards, kale, or mustard greens, washed well, tough stems removed and discarded
1 tablespoon of fresh lemon juice
1 teaspoon of salt and 1/4 teaspoon of freshly ground pepper to taste

(for garnish)

extra olive oil, lemon wedges, grated hard, cooked egg, if desired

SERVES 4

IN THE GOOD OLD SUMMERTIME—CORN IS KING

There is hardly a vegetable more American than corn, but it wasn't always the sweet table corn-on-the-cob we savor today. The Iroquois Indians referred to corn, beans, and squashes as "the three sisters." In the restored colonial village at Plymouth, Massachusetts, a demonstration planting showed how the three plants were sown, with the growing characteristic of each one benefiting the other. Corn was planted first. As it grew, beans were planted. The corn stalk supported the bean vines and they wound around the stalk. Corn seeds were planted about three feet apart and the squash or pumpkin was planted in-between. The three sisters constituted the basic Indian diet in both of the Americas.

The hard Indian corn kernels were scraped off the cob using a simple indigenous tool which was, according to food historian Peter Rose, a deer jawbone. The corn was then ground by hand or soaked in ash or lime water and hulled before it was usable for making into various dishes.

Christopher Columbus was the first European to discover maize (the proper name for corn) as well as squash and beans—in Cuba. He sent seeds back to Europe but it never became popular there except for polenta in Italy. Maize is the only cereal and food plant that needs man to help it reproduce. For years, researchers have tried to develop a self-seeding corn. The tight shuck around the kernels prevent them from making contact with the soil. Planting corn transformed nomadic Indian tribes into more settled communities as they waited for their corn to mature.

Only 1% of all the corn grown is sweet table corn. The rest is animal food or made into cornstarch, corn syrup, cornmeal, corn oil products, breakfast cereals, whiskey, and yes, popcorn. There are hundreds of known corn varieties. Sweet corn, although known to be grown by some Iroquois Indians at the beginning of the 17th century in central New York, was discovered in 1799 but wasn't widely cultivated until after the Civil War. It was actually the early 1920s before seeds were available to home gardeners, when corn's popularity grew quickly. It must be the favorite vegetable of all children, whether fresh, frozen, or canned. But we aspire to the expression, "fresh is best."[1,2]

Freeze a large batch of corn-on-the-cob the modern way.

Linda Neill in Ft. Pierce, Florida, whose husband is a farmer, passed along this simple way to prepare corn for the home freezer: Husk and desilk the corn. Lay it in the top and bottom racks of your dishwasher. Let it go through the rinse and dry cycles. (Without soap, of course.) Remove the corn, then immediately dip the ears in ice water, bag them, and place them directly into the freezer.

Footnotes

1-Culinary Historian Peter Rose, lecture, 1999, James McNair's *Corn* cookbook, 1990, *Food* by Waverly Root, 1980. Visit to Plimoth Plantation.

2-See also in this series the *Pumpkin Companion* by Elizabeth Brabb with Bruce T.

Paddock for the complete history of pumpkins and Native American agriculture, p12.

QUICK CORN RELISH

(1) Combine corn kernels with onion, and the green and red peppers in a large pyrex glass bowl.

(2) Combine corn cooking liquid with vinegar, oil, sugar, dry mustard, salt, pepper, and hot pepper flakes in a small saucepan. Bring to a boil.

(3) Pour hot liquid over vegetables. Cover with plastic wrap. Cool, then refrigerate overnight, stirring occasionally. Serve as a side dish at a picnic or barbecue or as a relish with sandwiches.

 INGREDIENTS

1/2 cup of corn cooking liquid (saved from cooking the corn)

3 cups of cooked corn kernels (cut from about 6 medium ears)

2/3 cup of diced onion

2/3 cup of diced green pepper

2/3 cup of diced red sweet pepper

1/2 cup of white vinegar

2 tablespoons of vegetable oil

1/2 cup of sugar

2 teaspoons of dry mustard

12 teaspoon of salt

1/2 teaspoon of freshly ground black pepper

1/2 teaspoon of hot pepper flakes (optional)

MAKES ABOUT 5 CUPS OF RELISH

CURRIED CREAM OF CORN SOUP

(1) In a 2-quart pan melt the butter and add the onions and garlic. Sauté on low until transparent and just starting to turn golden.

(2) Add the curry and chili powders and stir well. Set aside.

(3) Put the corn kernels and 1/4 cup of water into a food processor or blender and process or blend for a minute or two or until fairly smooth.

(4) Place a medium-fine strainer over a bowl and pour the corn mixture in. With the back of a wooden spoon or a spatula, mash to exude the liquid. You will have about 1 1/2 cups of corn cream liquid. Discard the pulp.

(5) Add the corn cream to the curry base along with the 1 cup of the chicken broth. Stir well. At this point the mixture can be refrigerated to use within 2 to 3 days.

(6) Heat corn soup over medium heat and gradually add 1/3 cup of cream to the consistency you desire. Heat through and season with salt and pepper.

(7) Pour into 4 bowls, garnish with greenery of choice.

 INGREDIENTS

4 tablespoons of sweet butter
1/2 cup of minced onion
1 teaspoon of minced garlic
2 teaspoons of curry powder or to taste
1 teaspoon of chili powder or to taste (optional)
3 cups of cooked corn kernels
1/4 cup of water
1-1 1/2 cups of chicken broth
1/3 cup of heavy cream
salt and pepper to taste
chopped dill, scallions, or cilantro for garnish

NOTE: *The soup may also be lightened by adding remaining stock. This soup can be served hot or cold.*

SERVES 4

FARMHOUSE
CUCUMBER SALAD

(1) Place cucumber slices in a colander, sprinkle with salt and toss together.
(2) Place colander over a plate to catch released liquid and let stand at least an hour.
(3) Pour cucumber slices into a glass bowl and add the onion. Toss to mix.
(4) Whisk together the mayonnaise, vinegar, and milk until smooth. Pour over cucumbers and toss well. Allow to stand for a few minutes and toss again. Sprinkle with freshly ground black pepper to taste. Serve garnished with chopped chives.

 INGREDIENTS

4 medium-sized cucumbers, peeled and sliced thin
1 teaspoon of salt, preferably Kosher style
1/2 medium onion, finely diced
1 cup of mayonnaise, regular or low fat
1/4 cup of cider vinegar
1/4 cup of milk
1 tablespoon of chopped chives for garnish

SERVES 6-8

NOTE: *The Filasky (originally Filarski) farm functioned from 1890 through the 1950s in New Hyde Park, New York, 20 miles from Manhattan. Their produce was sent to the New York market but the family also ran a farmstand in the Depression ravished 1930s. This is Wilhelmina Filasky's recipe. It came to us through her granddaughter who has fond memories of growing up on the farm.*

ORIENTAL CUCUMBER SALAD

(1) Mix the salt, sugar, soy sauce, vinegar, and sesame seed oil together making sure the salt and sugar are dissolved.

(2) Pour over the cucumber slices, toss, mixing well; chill before serving.

 INGREDIENTS

2 medium cucumbers, peeled, cut lengthwise in half, seeded and sliced into 1/8-inch slices

DRESSING
1/4 teaspoon salt
1 teaspoon of superfine sugar
1 tablespoon of light soy sauce
1 tablespoon of rice vinegar
2 teaspoons of roasted sesame seed oil

SERVES 4

EGGPLANT WITH CURRIED
COUSCOUS FILLING

(1) Trim stem ends and cut eggplants lengthwise in half. Scoop out the pulp leaving a shell about 1/2 inch thick. Cut pulp into 1/2-inch dice. Lightly salt the shells and drain cut side down on paper towels until ready to use.

(2) Bring the broth to a boil in a small pan or in the microwave, add the couscous, remove from heat, cover and let stand for 5 minutes. Fluff lightly with a fork.

(3) Heat oil in a skillet, add onion and diced eggplant pieces and sauté over low heat until soft, about 15 minutes. Do not let brown. Add tomato, peppers, and cilantro; mix, and simmer another few minutes. Remove mixture to a bowl, add all remaining ingredients, including couscous, taste and adjust seasonings.

Preheat the oven to 300° F.

(4) Fill the eggplant shells with the mixture. Dot with bits of butter. Grease a baking dish, add broth or water to depth of about 1/4 inch and place the filled eggplant in the broth.

(5) Cover with foil and bake for 40 minutes, uncovering the dish the last ten minutes.

NOTE: This is a flavorsome and satisfying vegetarian main dish serving 4. As a side dish it serves 6-8

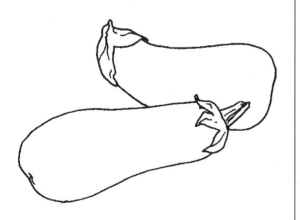

INGREDIENTS

2 medium-size eggplants
1/2 cup of chicken or vegetable
    broth + extra for baking pan
1/3 cup of quick cooking couscous
3 tablespoons of olive oil
2/3 cup of minced onion
1 very ripe tomato, peeled, seed-
    ed and diced
2 sweet red peppers, seeded and
    diced small
2 tablespoons of chopped
    cilantro
2 cloves of garlic, minced
2 teaspoons of fresh lemon juice
salt and pepper to taste
1 1/2 teaspoons of mild curry
    powder or to taste
1 tablespoon of chopped fresh
    mint leaves
butter for dotting stuffed eggplant
    and greasing baking dish

SERVES 4

ESCAROLE AND WHITE BEANS

(1) In a medium soup pot, heat the olive oil. Add garlic, onion, salt, pepper, and pepper flakes. Sauté about 5 minutes.

(2) Add escarole, cover, cook about 3 minutes or until escarole is limp.

(3) Uncover, cook until any remaining liquid evaporates.

(4) Add the beans. Heat thoroughly.

(5) Re-season with salt and pepper to taste.

(6) Transfer to a serving bowl and sprinkle with parsley, cheese, and a drizzle of olive oil. Serve as a side dish with roasted chicken or roasted meats.

NOTE: To make a hearty soup, add the beans with their liquid + 2 cups of chicken stock during the very last minutes of cooking. Heat thoroughly. Cooked elbow or shell pasta can also be added for substance. Serve this with grated Italian cheese of your choice, crispy bread, and a chilled Pinot Grigio.

 INGREDIENTS

1 head of escarole, rinsed, dried, coarsely chopped (about 8 cups, tightly packed)

3 tablespoons of olive oil

1 tablespoon of minced garlic

1/2 cup of minced onion

1 teaspoon of salt

1/2 teaspoon of pepper

1/4 teaspoon of hot pepper flakes

1 15-ounce can of cannelloni beans, drained

1/4 cup of minced flat leaf parsley

extra olive oil for drizzling

(for garnish)

1/2 cup grated cheese (optional)

SERVES 4

FENNEL, ARUGULA AND ORANGE
SALAD

(1) Make the dressing by combining the dressing ingredients and using the salt and pepper to your taste. Chill for at least 3 hours but it will hold a few days in the fridge.

(2) Rinse and remove the ferns from the top of the fennel and discard or use them in soup.

(3) Slice the fennel lengthwise into very thin slivers maintaining as much of the fennel shape as possible.

(4) Rinse the arugula well and tear into bite-sized pieces. Dry well.

(5) With a knife, peel the oranges and slice off as much of the membrane as you can, keeping the oranges intact. Slice the oranges into thin slices.

To Serve:

(6) Place some arugula on each of the 4 to 6 salad dishes. Lay the fennel slices on top of the arugula in a decorative pattern leaving the center free for the oranges.

(7) Place a few overlapping orange slices in the center of each dish.

(8) Drizzle on a bit of the salad dressing and serve.

 INGREDIENTS

SALAD:

1 large or 2 small bulbs of fennel
2 bunches of arugula
2 naval oranges

DRESSING:

3 tablespoons of good red wine vinegar
1/4 cup of orange juice
1/4 cup of extra-virgin olive oil
1 teaspoon of chopped fresh oregano or 1/2 teaspoon dried
1 teaspoon of Worcestershire sauce
salt and pepper to taste

NOTE: Double the dressing ingredients if you like a well-dressed salad.

SERVES 4-6

FENNEL WITH LAMB SHANKS

(1) In a heavy casserole or fry pan, heat the olive oil.

(2) Add the lamb and brown well on all sides, about 10 to 15 minutes.

(3) While the lamb is browning, cut the fennel bulb in quarters and coarsely chop. Add to the lamb shanks and sauté 5 minutes. Add the onion and salt and pepper to taste. Stir the vegetables together.

(4) Allow this mixture to brown until caramelized to a deep golden color. The deeper the color of the fennel and onion, the richer your sauce will be.

(5) Add the garlic, sauté three minutes then add 1 cup of liquid. Cover partially and simmer thirty minutes. Check from time to time. As liquid evaporates add more.

(6) After thirty minutes, add any remaining liquid and simmer, partially covered, until lamb is very tender and meat is just pulling away from the bone.

(7) Remove cover and cook until liquid thickens slightly to a sauce consistency.

(8) Re-season with salt and pepper to taste. Garnish with sprigs of fennel tops.

(9) Serve with Escarole and White Beans (page 60) or Peas with Onions in Acorn Squash Cups (page 77).

NOTE: *Fennel is a beautiful bulbous plant that has a distinctive anise flavor and aroma. Eaten raw it works wonders for the digestion. Dipped in olive oil with a bit of pepper mixed in provides you with a cooling appetizer. When cooked, the flavor of fennel intensifies. This recipe is an example of how a vegetable can add dimension to a less expensive cut of meat.*

 INGREDIENTS

4 lamb shanks
1 large head of fennel, feathery tops removed and reserved for garnish
1/4 cup of olive oil
1 medium onion, chopped
salt and pepper to taste
2 cloves of garlic, minced
1-2 cups of either chicken stock, white wine, or water

SERVES 4

GARLIC—THE FLAVOR ENHANCER AND CURATIVE

You might want to ward off vampires, decorate your kitchen, or maybe you just want to enhance a dish of sautéed spinach or escarole. Only a head of garlic, the enhancer of all time, will fit all those needs. The medicinal quality of garlic is legendary, from being a cure for bubonic plague to reducing high blood pressure and curing baldness. But most of us know it best for the flavoring it imparts to millions of dishes in cuisines all over the world. The aroma, the flavor, just the mention of garlic causes many a gland to salivate. Just sauté the garlic and they will come!

A member of the lily family, with its pungent odor and spicy flavor, garlic is closely related to the onion and the shallot. It can make or break a recipe depending on the amount used. When eaten in large doses it permeates the body and expels itself through the pores of the skin. That should be enough reason to use garlic in a discreet manner. But even with the possibility of losing a friend or two, garlic remains a constant ingredient, particularly in the cuisines of Italy and China. As the interest in ethnic cooking expands, the growing of garlic has proven to be a boon to many a farmer.

There are over 300 varieties of garlic cultivated all over the world. At any garlic festival you can choose from Spanish Roja, Carpathian from Central Europe, Romanian Red, Italian Red, Nootka Rose, and Northwest Heirloom from the San Juan Islands.

To select garlic, encircle a bulb in the palm of your hand and be sure that the cloves are firmly in place against each other. Press around the bulb and if you find air spaces you know you have old garlic. Tightness is the key.

HERB ROASTED
FRESH GARLIC

Preheat the oven to 375° F.

(1) Using a sharp knife slice off enough of the top of garlic to expose the pulp.

(2) Place garlic on the foil and drizzle olive oil over the top. Sprinkle with salt to taste and a generous amount of ground pepper.

(3) Sprinkle the herb of choice on top and wrap the foil around the garlic leaving just the top exposed.

(4) Place the garlic on a center rack in the oven and bake for 20 to 30 minutes or until top is golden and garlic is soft.

(5) Cool and serve warm or at room temperature spread on bread slices or tomato slices.

 INGREDIENTS

1 head of firm garlic (elephant garlic is appropriate but not as flavorful)

enough foil to wrap the garlic

2-3 tablespoons of virgin olive oil

salt and pepper to taste

chopped fresh herb of choice (oregano, rosemary, or basil) or 1 teaspoon of dried herbs (optional)

sliced bread or tomato to serve

SERVES 4 AS AN APPETIZER SPREAD

NOTE: The secret to using garlic is to use it gently. A little chopped garlic here, some sliced garlic there, and if you really want a garlic fix, roast a whole head and squeeze the pulp onto slices of crusty French or Italian bread and drizzle on some good olive oil. If you check some of your older cookbooks you will probably not find any recipes for garlic by itself but the trend now is to appreciate garlic not just as an enhancer but as an ingredient flavor unto itself.

KALE WITH PINKELWURST

(1) Remove and discard any tough stems from the kale. Stack up the leaves and cut into 1/2-inch strips. Cut the strips in half. Set aside.

(2) Heat the oil in a large pot and sauté the onion until transparent. Add the kale strips, 1 teaspoon of salt, and the pinkelwurst pieces.

(3) Add 1 1/2 cups of water. Bring to a boil, reduce the heat, cover and cook slowly for about 1 hour, stirring occasionally. The kale should get very tender. Cook longer, if necessary. Taste and add more salt, if desired and a grinding of fresh pepper.

(4) When kale is tender, remove cover and let any excess liquid evaporate. The oatmeal in the pinkelwurst will thicken most of the liquid. Serve hot.

 INGREDIENTS

1 pound of fresh kale, washed well in plenty of cool water
1 large onion, chopped
2 tablespoons of olive or vegetable oil
2 ounces of pinkelwurst, casing removed and broken into pieces (available from a German-style meat market)
salt and pepper to taste

SERVES 4

NOTE: *Pinkelwurst is a German sausage that contains oatmeal. It adds a distinctive flavor to this dish. Cut off the amount called for in the recipe from the piece you buy and freeze the unused portion. It keeps for up to a year. You might try using kielbasa if pinkelwurst isn't available. Traditionally kale is a fall vegetable as the first frost destroyed insects the curly leaves might harbor. Today, kale is available year round.*

CREAMED KOHLRABI
WITH TARRAGON

(1) Peel each globe, slice into 1/2-inch slices, then 1/2-inch strips, and finally 1/2-inch cubes.

(2) Place kohlrabi cubes into an appropriate size pan, cover with water, add salt to taste and bring to a boil. Reduce heat, cover and simmer for 15 minutes or until fork tender.

(3) Drain, saving the liquid for other sauces or soup, and place kohlrabi into a serving bowl. Spoon the following cream sauce over the top and serve piping hot.

Cream Sauce in the Microwave;

(1) Place butter in a 2-cup glass measure and melt in microwave on medium-high, 30 seconds to one minute. Stir in flour and heat on medium for 30 seconds. Stir.

(2) Whisk in milk, salt, and pepper. Heat on high for 1 minute. Stir, then heat on medium, 1 minute at a time, until sauce thickens. Stir and add snipped tarragon.

NOTE: *Be sure to select fresh young kohlrabi, available particularly in the spring and fall. As it ages, it becomes woody and fibrous—even after long cooking, it will remain firm.*

 INGREDIENTS

1 1/4 pounds of kohlrabi globes, each no more than 3 inches in diameter

salt to taste for cooking water

CREAM SAUCE

1 1/2 tablespoons of butter or margarine

1 1/2 tablespoons of all-purpose flour

3/4 cup milk, whole or reduced fat

1/2 teaspoon of salt

1/8 teaspoon of white pepper

1 tablespoon of snipped fresh tarragon leaves or 1 1/2 teaspoons dehydrated*

cooking liquid from kohlrabi as needed

*1/4 teaspoon of freshly grated nutmeg may be substituted for the tarragon.

SERVES 4

THREE-MUSHROOM SOUP

(1) Cut a piece of waxed paper or parchment paper to the size of a large skillet. Butter or oil the paper and set aside.

(2) Melt the butter or margarine in the skillet and add the chopped scallions. Cover with the oiled paper (oiled side on mushrooms) and the skillet lid. On low heat, cook or "sweat" the scallions just until tender, about five minutes. Remove the paper.

(3) Add the chopped mushrooms and cook, stirring, for 2 minutes.

(4) Add the 2 tablespoons of flour and cook, stirring, for 3 minutes.

(5) Remove pan from heat and add the heated milk and stock in a stream, using a whisk to gently blend all ingredients.

(6) Return to heat, bring to a boil, and simmer for 5 minutes, stirring. Add salt and pepper to taste.

(7) Serve garnished with chopped parsley or scallions, if you prefer.

NOTE: *This has a fresh, delicious flavor.*

 INGREDIENTS

3 tablespoons of unsalted butter or margarine

3/4 cup of chopped scallions; use some of the green tops

2 cups of chopped mushrooms; a combination of white, shiitake, and crimini

2 tablespoons of flour

1 cup of milk* and 1 cup of chicken stock, heated together

salt and freshly ground white pepper, to taste

2 tablespoons of chopped parsley for garnish

You may use low-fat or skim milk. To add creaminess, use part evaporated skim milk.

SERVES 4

MUSHROOM SALAD

(1) In a glass bowl, combine mushrooms, celery, green pepper, red onion, and roasted pepper.

(2) In another bowl, combine red wine vinegar, garlic, Worcestershire sauce, and salt. Whisk in vegetable oil in a steady stream.

(3) Toss mushroom mixture with dressing. Serve "as is" or on a large lettuce leaf as part of a salad plate, garnished with chopped parsley.

 INGREDIENTS

1 1/2 cups of white button mushrooms, cut into 1/16-inch slices
1/2 cup of finely diced celery
1/4 cup of diced green pepper
1/4 cup of diced red onion
1/4 cup of diced roasted red pepper or pimiento
2 teaspoons of red wine vinegar
1 clove of garlic, minced
1/4 teaspoon of Worcestershire sauce
1/4 teaspoon of salt
3 tablespoons of vegetable oil
chopped parsley for garnish

MAKES 4 SERVINGS

ONIONS

Onions are sweet, spicy, juicy, and one of the most essential ingredients in food preparation. Sauté them, fry them, roast them, bake them, grill them, or boil them—no matter how onions are prepared they hold their own and enhance at the same time. Onions are one of the main coloring agents in a good brown stock. For a deeply colored stock they are halved and char-blackened on the cut-side before being added to the stock pot or they are added skin intact for a more subtle shading. The color and shape of the onion was immortalized in 1881 by Pierre Auguste Renoir in his painting simply entitled, "Onions." It now hangs in the Sterling and Francine Clark Institute in Williamstown, Massachusetts.

ONION SOUP THE FRENCH WAY

(1) In a large heavy stock pot, melt the butter and sauté the onions until golden brown allowing some to stick to the bottom of the pan and turn brown.

(2) When well browned, stir in the stock and garlic and simmer for 30 minutes.

(3) Season to taste with salt and pepper. Turn the heat off.

Preheat the oven to 375° F.

(4) Place two slices of bread in each bowl.

(5) Ladle the soup slowly into the crocks so that the bread absorbs the soup. Fill each bowl to the top.

(6) Sprinkle cheese generously on top and around the edges.

(8) Bake until golden and crusty, about 30 minutes.

 INGREDIENTS

4 tablespoons of sweet butter
6 cups of thinly sliced onions
10 cups of chicken stock or beef stock
2 cloves of garlic, minced very fine
salt and pepper to taste
12-16 1-inch thick slices of French bread, lightly toasted
1 pound of French Gruyère cheese, shredded
6-8 onion soup crocks or oven-proof soup bowls

SERVES 6-8 DEPENDING UPON SIZE OF SOUP BOWLS

VIDALIA ONION FOCACCIA
WITH GORGONZOLA AND WALNUTS

(1) Slow-cook (caramelize) the onions with oil and butter in a 10-inch skillet over very low heat for 45-60 minutes. Stir every 5 minutes or so. They should not brown, just become tender and glossy. Make crust dough (recipe follows) while onions cook.

NOTE: *Caramelized onions with some chopped thyme or tarragon and a little salt and pepper make a delicious side dish.*

Dough;

(1) Combine 1 1/2 cups of flour, salt, and yeast in a large bowl or electric mixer. Heat water and olive oil to 125-130° F. Add to dry ingredients.
(2) Beat 2 minutes at low speed, scraping bowl occasionally. Beat 2 minutes at high speed. Stir in enough additional flour to make a soft dough. (You may not use all 3 1/2 cups of flour.)
(3) Turn out dough on a lightly floured surface and knead about 4-6 minutes, until dough is smooth and elastic. Use more flour, as needed, to prevent sticking.
(4) Clean the mixing bowl and rinse with very hot water. Dry, and invert the bowl over your dough, letting the dough rest for 15 or 20 minutes in this warm environment.

Preheat the oven to 400° F.

(6) Spread the 1 tablespoon of olive oil in a 10x15-inch jelly-roll pan. Place the dough in the pan and pat and press with your fingers until it fills the entire pan and has a rimmed edge. Pierce the dough surface evenly with a fork and make small indents with a finger or handle of a wooden spoon. Bake for 5 minutes and remove from oven.
(7) Cover partially baked crust evenly with the caramelized onions. Sprinkle with the rosemary, gorgonzola, and toasted walnuts.
(8) Bake for 20 minutes or until golden brown. Serve warm, cut into squares or rectangles.

NOTE: *If you're traveling through Georgia in the spring, the local farmstands feature bags of delicious, sweet Vidalia onions. They also appear in local markets everywhere. Germany, France, and Italy all have their own versions of an onion pie. Here's one that uses these sweet native Georgia onions. The focaccia bakes at 400° F. but don't preheat the oven yet. The onions take about 45 minutes to caramelize and the dough takes about 20 minutes before pressing into a pan, so start the onions first.*

*You may substitute red onions or other sweet onions for Vidalias if they are unavailable.
**Toast walnuts in a small pan until lightly browned.

 INGREDIENTS

TOPPING
3 large Vidalia onions (about 2 pounds)*
3/8 pound of crumbled Gorgonzola cheese, cut into lengthwise slivers
cheese (Feta)
2 tablespoons of olive oil
1 tablespoon of butter
1 cup of coarsely chopped, toasted walnuts**
3 tablespoons of fresh rosemary leaves

DOUGH
3 1/2 cups of all-purpose flour
1 cup of water
3/4 teaspoon of salt
3 tablespoons of olive oil
1 package of regular or Rapid Rise yeast
1 tablespoon olive oil for the pan

MAKES 1 10x15-INCH FOCACCIA OR 8-10 APPETIZER PORTIONS OR 4-6 MAIN DISH PORTIONS

ROASTED ONION RINGS

(1) Line a round or rectangular baking sheet or pan with tin foil. Lightly coat with the olive oil.
(2) Peel and slice the onions into 1/4 to 1/2-inch rings. Separate the rings and spread them out in the pan. (Keep the rings as separate as possible to avoid a steamed final product.)
(3) Sprinkle with salt and pepper to taste.

Preheat the oven to 400° F.

(4) Place in the upper portion of the oven and bake 20 to 30 minutes or until the rings are crisp and brown. Move the onions around in the pan to facilitate an even browning.
(5) When done to your liking, place on some paper toweling and serve either as a side dish or as a garnish on meats, fish, or salad.

NOTE: *For variation, sprinkle with fresh or dried herbs, chili powder, or curry powder.*

 INGREDIENTS

2 large onions, thinly sliced (Vidalia, Spanish, or red)
2 tablespoons of olive oil
salt and pepper to taste

NOTE: *If you love fried onion rings but are concerned about the amount of oil you're ingesting you'll love this recipe. It works well with any onion, but it is most succulent when the sweet, spring, vidalia onion is used. The rings are brown and crisp and when piled high will form a tower over burgers, steak, grilled chicken, or even a salad. Try them once and they will become a standby in your repertoire.*

SERVES 2-4 DEPENDING ON

PARSNIP PURÉE

(1) Cut the parsnip into 1-inch pieces and cook in boiling water (to which has been added 1/2 teaspoon of the salt) until fork tender, only about 5-8 minutes.

(2) Drain—saving the liquid for soups or to thin puréed parsnip if too thick—and turn the parsnip into a food processor, along with the other 1/2 teaspoon of salt, soft butter, cream, dry sherry, and maple syrup. Purée the mixture. Taste and adjust seasonings

(3) Scrape into an appropriate-sized oven-proof casserole, top with the bread crumbs and nuts, and dot with the 2 teaspoons of butter. Bake at 350° F. for about 20 minutes, until crumbs and nuts are lightly browned.

NOTE *If preparing ahead and refrigerating, bring to room temperature before baking and add a few more minutes to the oven time. This is a nice accompaniment to poultry and pork.*

 INGREDIENTS

1-1 1/2 pounds of parsnips, peeled
1 teaspoon of salt, divided
1 tablespoon of soft butter
1 tablespoon of light cream or fat-free Half-and-Half
2 tablespoons of dry sherry
1 teaspoon of pure maple syrup
1 tablespoon of dry, plain bread crumbs
1 tablespoon of finely chopped almonds or pecans
2 teaspoons of butter for dotting top of casserole

NOTE: *James Beard felt that parsnips were a delicious but often ignored root vegetable. I wouldn't dream of making vegetable soup without a parsnip. It is probably one of the most naturally sweet vegetables of all. Add a cooked parsnip to potatoes when mashing, for a flavor treat. They cook fast so don't overcook.*

SERVES 3-4

GINGERY CANDIED PARSNIPS

(1) Peel the parsnips and slice into 1/4-inch rounds.
(2) Bring 3 inches of water to a boil in a 3-quart pan; add 1/2 teaspoon of salt and the parsnip slices. Simmer for 7-9 minutes or until the slices are fork tender. Don't overcook. Drain, saving the cooking liquid for soup or vegetable stock.
(3) In a large skillet, melt the butter over low heat. Stir in the brown sugar, ginger, and salt. When the sugar/butter mixture starts to bubble, add the cooked parsnip slices in a single layer, turning each slice several times to coat with the sugar mixture. Let them cook gently for 7 or 8 minutes to "candy" them.

 INGREDIENTS

2 parsnips, 9-11 ounces each, 2 inches wide at the base
1/2 teaspoon of salt for cooking the parsnips
3 tablespoons of butter
1/4 cup of dark brown sugar
1 teaspoon of finely grated fresh ginger root
1/2 teaspoon of salt

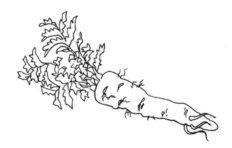

SERVES 4-5

PEAS WITH ONIONS IN ACORN SQUASH CUPS

(1) Brush the inside and outside of the acorn cups with 1/8 cup of the oil.

Preheat the oven to 375° F.

(2) Line a medium baking dish with tin foil and place the cups onto the foil. Add 1/2 cup of water to the pan. Bake until tender, about 30 to 45 minutes. Test for tenderness by piercing the pulp with a fork. Remove from the oven and keep warm.

(3) Heat 1/8 cup of the oil in a sauté pan and add the onions. Add the peas on top and sprinkle with salt and pepper to taste.

(4) Cover and cook over a medium heat for about 15 minutes.

(5) After first 5 minutes combine the peas and onions and continue cooking for 10 minutes.

(6) Remove cover and sauté until any remaining liquid has evaporated, peas are tender, and onion is slightly browned, about 15 minutes. Stir frequently.

(7) Re-season with salt and pepper and portion evenly into the acorn squash cups.

 INGREDIENTS

2 medium acorn squash, halved horizontally to form cups, seeded
1/4 cup of canola or corn oil
1 large sweet onion, peeled, thinly sliced
1 pound of shelled fresh peas (2 pounds unshelled)
salt and pepper to taste

NOTE: *Serve with roasts, steaks, or Fennel with Lamb Shanks (see page 62). These can also be assembled ahead of time and reheated.*

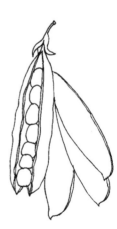

SERVES 4

TRI-COLORED PEPPER SALAD
WITH ORANGE MUSTARD DRESSING

For the Dressing;

(1) Blend garlic, cilantro, orange juice, vinegar, zest, and mustard well, adding oil and vinegar last. Keep chilled.

For the Salad;

(1) Combine the carrots, yellow peppers, red peppers, scallions, and onion; toss with the Orange Mustard Dressing.
(2) Add salt and pepper to taste. Keep chilled.

INGREDIENTS

DRESSING
1 tablespoon of minced garlic
1 tablespoon of chopped cilantro
1/4 cup of orange juice
1 tablespoon of orange zest
2 tablespoons of whole grain mustard
1/4 cup of olive oil
1/4 cup of rice wine vinegar
salt and pepper to taste

SALAD
2 large carrots, shredded
2 yellow peppers, julienned
2 sweet red peppers, julienned
1 bunch scallions, julienned
1/2 red onion, julienned
1 recipe Orange Mustard Dressing (see above)
salt and pepper to taste

SERVES 2-4

BAKED POTATO BAR

Preheat the oven to 375° F.

(1) Bake Idaho or russet potatoes for about 60 minutes, sweet potatoes about 50 minutes, or until a sharp fork pierces them easily and they are soft to the squeeze.

(2) Cut a large "X" into each hot potato, squeeze them partially open and set them out on a large platter or hot tray, (sprinkle some paprika on the white potatoes) surrounded by the various toppings.

NOTE: *If you're having a crowd, try a Baked Potato Bar as part of your buffet. Your guests can pick and choose the toppings they like from the following suggestions:*
    Butter or margarine
    Sour cream and caviar
    Chopped scallions, chives, and parsley
    Tiny cooked broccoli flowerets
    Grated Cheddar or Parmesan

 INGREDIENTS

Idaho or russet baking potatoes—1 per person, scrubbed and pierced with a fork

A few sweet potatoes or yams, scrubbed and pierced with a fork

NOTE: *(continued)*
    Basil pesto
    Cooked chopped spinach
    Salsa
    Diced avocado
    Crumbled crisp bacon bits
    Diced prosciutto or ham
    Hot stewed tomatoes
    Baked garlic
    Brown sugar for the sweet potatoes
    Paprika for garnish

SERVES 1 POTATO PER PERSON

POTATO DUMPLINGS
(KARTOFFEL KLOSSE)

(1) Early in the day you plan to make the dumplings, or the day before, boil the potatoes, in their skins, until done—about 25-30 minutes. Set aside the cooked potatoes to cool and dry out. Pierce them a couple of times with a fork.

(2) When ready to make the dumplings, peel the potatoes and put them through a potato ricer or grate them. It's easier if you cut each one in half first. You should have 3 cups of riced potatoes.

(3) Add the flour, farina, egg yolks, parsley, nutmeg, and salt. Mix together thoroughly. If the mixture seems too dry, add a little of the egg white and mix.

(4) Flour your hands and roll the mixture into 8 uniformly round dumplings. Each will be about the size of a lime.

(5) Bring a large pot of water to a boil (5-quart pot). Add 2 teaspoons of salt and gently drop in the dumplings. Keep the water at a bare simmer and let the dumplings simmer for about 15 minutes.

(6) Remove dumplings with a slotted spoon to a warm platter and top with sautéed, buttered Ritz cracker crumbs*. Serve with pot roast, sauerbraten, chicken fricassee, or any roast that has a sauce or gravy.

* Crumble about 10 Ritz crackers into 2 tablespoons of butter melted in a skillet. As the crumbs sauté, stir occasionally until they brown, nice and crisp.

NOTE: *Leftover dumplings are delicious sliced and sautéed in butter.*

NOTE: *These dumplings are basic fare in the kitchen of a German family. Although there are mixes and pre-pared dumplings you just drop into boiling water, there is something very satisfying about successfully making them from scratch. They are so good with buttered cracker crumbs and gravy!*

 INGREDIENTS

1 pound of baking potatoes such as Idaho or russets (3 medium potatoes)
2 tablespoons of flour
2 tablespoons of farina or matzo meal
2 egg yolks
2 tablespoons of minced parsley
1/4 teaspoon of freshly grated nutmeg
3/4 teaspoon of salt
1 egg-white as needed if mixture is dry

MAKES 8 DUMPLINGS

SWEET YUKON GOLD
POTATO PANCAKES

(1) Into a medium bowl, shred-grate the potatoes and onion.

(2) With a fork, stir in the flour and the pepper to taste. Blend well.

(3) In a heavy fry pan, heat enough oil to just coat the pan.

(4) When the oil is hot, spoon a portion of the potato mix onto the pan. Use enough to make a small patty. Press down with a spatula and allow to cook through until golden on the bottom side. Turn and cook another minute or two.

(5) Drain on a paper towel and serve hot with any pork dish or pot roast. Accompany with apple sauce.

NOTE: For hors d'oeuvres, mix some tiny diced green or red pepper cubes into the potato mix. Cook as directed and serve on a tray with applesauce or mustard for dipping.

 INGREDIENTS

2 medium Yukon Gold potatoes, peeled

1 medium yam or sweet potato, unpeeled

1 small purple potato, peeled (optional)

1 small onion, peeled

1/4 cup of flour

freshly ground pepper

oil for frying

MAKES 8 POTATO PANCAKES

KATHERINE'S MASHED POTATOES WITH
PROSCIUTTO AND MOZZARELLA

(1) Peel and cut the potatoes into 2-3-inch pieces.

(2) Place the potato pieces in a pot with salted water to cover and bring to a boil. Boil until potatoes are tender, about 20 minutes.

(3) Dice the prosciutto and mozzarella into 2-inch pieces and set aside.

(4) When the potatoes are done, tender to a fork, drain and put back into the pot.

(5) Add 4 tablespoons of butter and 1/2 cup milk. Mash with a fork or a masher.

(6) When creamy as you like, (add more butter or milk if necessary) add the prosciutto and mozzarella, mixing well.

(7) Season with salt and pepper to taste and turn into a soufflé dish or casserole dish that is just large enough to hold the potatoes in a mound extending above the rim of the dish.

(8) At this point you can keep out for a few hours until ready to bake or you can cover and keep chilled until baking time. Will hold this way for up to 3 days.

 INGREDIENTS

8 medium potatoes, rinsed (Russet, Long Island, Idaho, Golden Yukon)
4-6 tablespoons of butter
1/2-1 cup of milk
1/4 pound of prosciutto
1 pound of mozzarella (fresh if possible)
salt and pepper to taste

Preheat the oven to 350° F.

(9) Bake the potatoes for up to 1 hour, testing to be sure they are heated in the center. The potatoes will puff and become golden on top. Serve immediately.

SERVES 4-6

PUMPKIN BISQUE

(1) Heat butter and oil in a 3-quart pot over low heat. Add shallot, celery, onion, leeks, and carrot. Cook until the onions are translucent, stirring occasionally.

(2) Add pumpkin purée and chicken stock, cinnamon stick, nutmeg, and ginger slices. Bring to a boil over medium heat and simmer until vegetables are tender, about 20 minutes.

(3) Remove cinnamon stick and purée in batches, in processor or blender.

(4) Return puréed soup to pot, add maple syrup, salt, and milk. Return to a simmer, adding back the cinnamon stick. Thin soup with stock or water, if necessary.

(5) Serve piping hot, garnished with a few currants and a few pieces of almonds.

NOTE: *Talk to the pumpkin growers at your local farmstand and ask them which pumpkin variety is best for cooking and how to cook it. Whether you use fresh or canned pumpkin, it's full of antioxidents and makes a delicious soup.*

 INGREDIENTS

1 tablespoon of butter and 1 table-spoon of vegetable oil
1 shallot, finely diced
2/3 cup of finely diced celery
1/2 cup of finely diced onion
1/2 cup of chopped leeks, white part only
1 carrot, peeled and diced
2 1/2 cups of pumpkin purée, (freshly cooked, drained, and mashed)
1 quart of chicken stock
1 cinnamon stick
1/4 teaspoon of freshly grated nutmeg
1 piece of fresh ginger, 1/2x1-inch, peeled and sliced thin
2 tablespoons of maple syrup
1 teaspoon of salt
1 1/2 cups of evaporated skim milk

(for garnish)

2 tablespoons of dried currants
2 tablespoons of chopped, toasted almonds

SERVES 10

CANDIED PUMPKIN CHIPS

(1) Using the next to finest side of a four-sided grater, zest all the lemons onto waxed paper. After zesting, juice the lemons and strain the juice. Set aside.

(2) Combine pumpkin slices, ginger, sugar, lemon zest, and lemon juice in a medium saucepan. Slowly bring to a boil, stirring gently.

(3) Cook over low heat until pumpkin is almost translucent and retains some of its crunch (about 15-20 minutes). Using a slotted spoon, remove pumpkin from the syrup to a pyrex bowl.

(4) Continue to boil the syrup until slightly thickened, approximately 15-20 minutes longer. Don't overcook. Ladle syrup over pumpkin slices. Cover and let cool, then refrigerate. Serve with roast poultry or pork.

NOTE: From Robert Curry, Chef, The Chandon Club, Napa Valley, Ca.

 INGREDIENTS

3 lemons
1 Meyer lemon, if available (see note)
2 cups of pumpkin slices, 1/8-inch thick by 1-inch square (get pie pumpkin at a farm-stand)
2 ounces of crystallized ginger, roughly chopped
2 1/2 cups of sugar

NOTE: Meyer lemons are seasonal and are not as sour as regular lemons. If unavailable, substitute by adding 1/4 cup of orange juice to the strained lemon juice in step 1.

MAKES 6–8 SIDE SERVINGS

RHUBARB CITRUS CONSERVE

(1) Prepare rhubarb. Place in a 3-quart pan. Peel oranges and the lime thinly, using a vegetable peeler. Cut the peel into very, very thin strips. You should have 2 tablespoons of orange peel strips and 1 1/2 teaspoons of lime peel strips.

(2) Squeeze the juice from the oranges and the lime. You will need 1/2 cup of orange juice and 1 tablespoon of lime juice.

(3) Add the peels, juices, sugar, cranberries, and walnuts to the rhubarb. Over high heat, bring mixture to a boil, stirring constantly. Reduce heat but continue to boil, stirring regularly, for about 30 to 45 minutes, until mixture thickens or until a small amount dropped into a dish starts to gel.

(4) While mixture is cooking, sterilize 4 half-pint jars and their lids by boiling for 10 minutes (you can use recycled jelly jars). Fill the jars with the conserve and screw on the lids. Label and refrigerate. Use on toast, ice cream, or on custard. It's also a pleasing accompaniment to roast chicken or turkey.

 INGREDIENTS

2 pounds of rhubarb, cleaned, leaves removed, then chopped to yield 6 cups
2 large oranges
1 lime
3 cups of sugar
1/2 cup of dried cranberries or raisins
1/2 cup of coarsely chopped walnuts

NOTE: *Adapted from a Kerr Kitchen Pantry Newsletter,* The Rhubarb Issue. *Rhubarb is a vegetable that has been traced back as far as 2700 B.C. when it was used mainly medicinally. It's lovely red stalks are available at farmstands in the spring and it's tart flavor is unique. Never use the leaves as they are poisonous.*

MAKES 2 PINTS OR 4 HALF PINTS

GERMAN SPINACH

(1) Wash spinach well in a sink full of cold water. Drain.

(2) Prepare spinach by breaking off the stem. (If using baby spinach, there is no need to remove stems.) Coarsely chop.

(3) In a large pot with a cover, steam spinach with a small amount of water no more than five minutes.

(4) Meanwhile, cook the bacon pieces until crisp. Pour off the bacon fat, and drain the bacon on paper toweling.

(5) Without washing the pan, add the butter and sauté the shallots until translucent. Remove pan from heat and blend in the flour. Return pan to medium heat and let butter and flour mixture bubble up.

(6) Add the spinach to the pan with the shallots, making sure there is only a little liquid left in the pot. Let it bubble up and thicken. Add the bacon pieces, grate the fresh nutmeg over all, and serve hot.

 INGREDIENTS

1 pound of fresh spinach

2 strips of bacon, cut into 1/4-inch dice

2 shallots, diced fine or 2 tablespoons of finely diced onion

1 tablespoon of butter

1 tablespoon of flour

salt and pepper to taste

1/4 teaspoon of freshly grated nutmeg

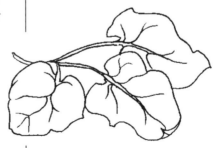

SERVES 4

SPINACH-LENTIL SOUP
WITH PASTA

(1) In a medium kettle or non-reactive pot, heat the olive oil and add the garlic. Simmer until barely golden.

(2) Add the oregano, pepper flakes, onion, carrots, and celery. Stir to coat the vegetables and simmer another 5 minutes.

(3) Add the lentils and stir to coat them with the oil. Simmer another 5 minutes.

(4) Add 8 cups of water and stir well. Partially cover and simmer over a low to medium heat for 30 minutes, stir occasionally. Test the lentils for creaminess and add more water if necessary.

(5) Continue to simmer until lentils are tender and creamy. Add water if you prefer a thinner soup.

(6) Season with salt and pepper to your taste. Stir in the spinach, simmer about 5 more minutes. Remove from the heat and serve immediately or reheat whenever ready to serve.

(7) Add some pasta to each soup bowl then ladle on the soup.

 INGREDIENTS

2 cups of lentils, rinsed, picked over for small stones

1/4 cup of olive oil

1 large clove of garlic, minced

1 teaspoon of oregano

1/4 teaspoon of hot pepper flakes (optional)

1/2 cup each of diced onion, carrots, and celery

salt and pepper to taste

2 cups of raw spinach, rinsed, drained, coarsely chopped

1 cup of small pasta, cooked, drained and tossed with a bit of olive oil to keep from sticking.

NOTE: Accompany with crusty Italian bread and a chilled dry white wine.

SERVES 4

TOMATOES

It's almost impossible to conceive our twenty-first century cuisine without tomatoes; no spaghetti sauce, no pizza, no bacon, lettuce, and tomato sandwiches, no tomato salad with basil, no stewed tomatoes, no tomato soup or ketchup or salsa. We like them fresh, canned, dried, grilled, baked, stewed, simmered, and broiled. This isn't always the way it was, however.

By the time Columbus arrived in the Americas, tomatoes had not yet reached the Caribbean Islands. Eventually, as more explorers ventured to the new world, tomato seeds arrived in Europe, likely first in Spain, at a time when Italy was under Spanish rule. These first tomato seeds brought to Europe produced a yellow fruit. The Italians took a fancy to the flavor, but only when cooked for hours. They thought death would ensue if they ate raw tomatoes since early botanists declared tomatoes to be poisonous. Yes, for years tomatoes had a bad reputation. In the late 1800s tomatoes were even accused of causing cancer.

In 1840 a daredevil named Colonel Robert Gibbon Johnson publicly ate a raw tomato. A crowd assembled to watch him die. Needless to say, he survived and tomato popularity was on its way in America. Early gardeners like Thomas Jefferson grew tomatoes ornamentally as early as 1781. Early recipes in England and the United States used the tomato for making various ketchups, a very cooked down, well-seasoned tomato purée.

Try to envision picking a small sun-warmed, red-ripe tomato fresh off the vine, sprinkling on a bit of salt and popping it into your mouth. You bite it and the warm juice squirts onto your tongue as you chew the tender morsel. That's a tomato!

NOTE: See Food by Waverley Root, The California Tomato Advisory Board, Cornell Cooperative Extension.

STUFFED TOMATOES

(1) Slice off the top of the tomatoes and core each with a spoon or sharp knife. Rinse and turn upside down on a piece of paper toweling to drain.

(2) In a small bowl, mix cheese, peppers, zucchini, sage, and pars-ley, salt and pepper to taste.

(3) Brush the tomato skin with some oil and fill with the mixture. Sprinkle extra cheese on top.

(4) Place on the grill and cook for 20 to 30 minutes or in an oven heated to 375° F. for 20 minutes until just soft with golden tops.

 INGREDIENTS

8 small to medium-sized tomatoes (about the size of red plums)

2 tablespoons of grated Pecorino or Romano cheese + extra for topping

1/2 cup each, small diced, green and red pepper

1/2 cup small diced zucchini

1 tablespoon each, minced sage and parsley

salt and pepper to taste

olive oil for brushing tomatoes

SERVES 4

OVEN OR SUN-DRIED
TOMATOES

(1) Wash the tomatoes and cut in half vertically. Sprinkle cut sides with salt.

(2) Place tomatoes on racks over jelly-roll pans lined with aluminum foil. Let the tomatoes stand on the counter for eight hours or overnight so the salt can draw out some of the tomato liquid. Pat the tomatoes dry.

(3) Place the racks of tomatoes in a 200° F. oven and bake for about 8 hours, turning the tomatoes once or twice. If no more liquid oozes out when you press with your finger, they are done. Do not over-cook.

(4) Lightly layer the dried tomatoes in sterile jars with olive oil, fresh basil leaves, chopped garlic, and black peppercorns, as desired.

(5) Alternatively, to dry in the sun, cover the racks with cheesecloth and set out in the full sun during the day. Return to the kitchen at night and place outside again on the second and perhaps third day, until dried. Then proceed to jarring as in step 4.

 INGREDIENTS

3 pounds of medium-sized plum tomatoes, red ripe and free of bruises
coarse salt
olive oil
fresh basil
garlic
black peppercorns

NOTE: *Adapted from a recipe by Marie Bianco, a food writer for Newsday.*

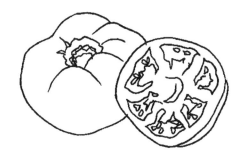

MAKES 1 JAR

SUN-DRIED TOMATO SPREAD

(1) Combine the tomatoes, basil, anchovies, capers, 2 tablespoons of olive oil, pepper, and almonds in a food processor or blender. Process until smooth.

(2) Spoon into a glass or ceramic jar and add a few tablespoons of olive oil to seal the top. Store in the refrigerator for up to one week.

NOTE: To serve, spread on crispy Italian bread toasts or stuff into the crevices of 2-inch celery stalks.

 INGREDIENTS

4 ounces of sun-dried tomatoes in oil (see Oven or Sun-Dried Tomatoes on page 91)

1 large basil leaf

4 anchovy filets

1 teaspoon of capers (optional)

2 tablespoons of extra-virgin olive oil + extra olive oil for storing purposes

black pepper to taste

1 tablespoon of slivered almonds (optional)

MAKES 1 JAR

BAKED TURNIP CASSEROLE

(1) Peel turnip, cut into 1-inch slices, then 1-inch strips and 1-inch cubes.

(2) In a medium-sized saucepan, cover the turnip cubes with water, add a teaspoon of salt and bring to a boil. Reduce heat, cover the pan and cook about 20 minutes or more, until turnip is tender when pierced with a sharp fork.

(3) While turnip is cooking, melt the butter in a small skillet and sauté the onion until tender. Stir in the flour. Set aside.

(4) Drain the turnip, saving some of the cooking liquid. Turn the turnip into a food processor bowl and process until no lumps of turnip remain, adding some of the cooking liquid, if needed. Add the brown sugar and mix briefly. Stir in the butter and onion mixture and turn into a greased casserole. Taste and add salt and pepper as needed. (Alternatively, use a quick prep, hand-held blender to mash the turnip.)

(5) Arrange the pieces of bacon evenly over the top of the turnip. Bake for 25 minutes or until bacon is crisp in a preheated 350° F. oven.

INGREDIENTS

1 medium turnip (1 1/2 pounds)
2 tablespoons of butter
1 small onion, finely minced
1 tablespoon of flour
1 teaspoon of dark brown sugar
salt and pepper to taste
2 strips bacon, each one cut
    into 3 pieces

NOTE: Great for Thanksgiving. It can be prepared ahead and baked when ready to serve. See Thanksgiving Cookery by James W. Baker and Elizabeth Brabb, pages 55-57 in this series.

NOTE: If you use yellow or white turnips, make sure they are heavy and firm. Light turnips may be woody, pithy, and strong-flavored.

SERVES 4-6

YUMMY YAM MUFFINS

Preheat the oven to 375° F.

(1) Lightly grease medium-size muffin pans for 12 muffins.

(2) Sift together into a large bowl, the flour, sugar, baking powder, salt, cinnamon, and nutmeg. Stir in the oatmeal and raisins.

(3) In a second bowl, beat together the egg, milk, margarine, and yam, until smooth.

(4) Add egg mixture to flour mixture, blending just until all the flour is incorporated. Fill muffin cups 2/3 full and bake for 20-25 minutes, until golden brown.

 INGREDIENTS

1 cup of all-purpose flour
1/3 cup of packed dark brown sugar
2 teaspoons of baking powder
1/2 teaspoon of salt
1/2 teaspoon of cinnamon
1/4 teaspoon of freshly grated nutmeg
1/2 cup of quick or regular oatmeal
1/3 cup of raisins or currants
1 egg
1/2 cup of low-fat milk
3 tablespoons of margarine or butter, melted
1/2 cup of cooked, mashed yam (1 small yam cooked, peeled and mashed)

MAKES 12 MEDIUM MUFFINS

TOFU STUFFED ZUCCHINI

(1) Wrap the tofu in paper toweling. Place a heavy weight on top for 10 minutes to squeeze out the extra moisture. (A heavy pan works well.)

(2) Wash the zucchini thoroughly and trim the ends. Slice them in half lengthwise. Scoop out the pulp, leaving a 1/4-inch shell. Chop the pulp and set aside.

(3) Sauté the onion and garlic in the vegetable oil until softened. Add the chopped zucchini, parsley, oregano, and peppers. Simmer over low heat for about 10 minutes, until zucchini is softened. Add more herbs if bland.

(4) Unwrap the tofu, blot any excess moisture you see and crumble it into small pieces. Add it to the zucchini mixture, blend and taste, adding more seasoning if desired. Remove from the heat and spoon into the reserved zucchini shells.

Preheat the oven to 350° F.

(5) Pour the tomato sauce into a glass baking dish—large enough for the four zucchini halves—and place the zucchini on top. Sprinkle with the Parmesan cheese.

 INGREDIENTS

1 12-ounce package of firm tofu
2 medium zucchini (about 7-8 ounces each)
2/3 cup of chopped onion
2 cloves of garlic, minced
2 tablespoons of vegetable oil
2 tablespoons of freshly chopped parsley
2 teaspoons of dried oregano
a pinch of hot pepper flakes
1/4 teaspoon of freshly ground pepper
2 cups of homemade fresh tomato sauce
1/4 cup of grated Romano cheese for topping

(6) Cover with foil and bake for 20 minutes. Remove foil and bake an additional 10 minutes or until zucchini is tender.

SERVES 4

ZUCCHINI PANCAKES

(1) Place the grated zucchini in a fine strainer over a bowl. Sprinkle with 1/2 teaspoon of the salt and let it sit at least 15 minutes; then press out as much fluid as possible, squeezing and/or pressing with paper toweling. Transfer to a mixing bowl. You should have about 2 cups of zucchini.

(2) Add the grated onion and stir in the beaten eggs, flour, baking powder, remaining salt, pepper to taste, grated nutmeg and wheat germ. Mix only until all ingredients are combined.

(3) Heat oil in a large skillet. When skillet is hot, use about 2 tablespoons of batter per pancake, flattening and shaping them into 3-4 inch rounds. Lightly brown on one side and turn to brown the other side. Drain on paper toweling and serve hot with sour cream or grated Parmesan.

INGREDIENTS

2 pounds of washed fresh zucchini, unpeeled, grated
1 teaspoon of salt, divided
1 medium onion, grated
2 eggs, beaten
1/2 cup of flour
a good pinch of baking powder
freshly ground pepper to taste
1/4 teaspoon of freshly grated nutmeg
2 tablespoons of wheat germ (optional)
1/4 cup of vegetable oil for frying
sour cream or freshly grated Parmesan cheese for serving

MAKES 14 PANCAKES

GRILLING VEGETABLES

To grill is to cook with direct heat on a grid of metal over an open flame. The heat is always intense. The ingredients cook quickly, and are often left with a seared and blackened surface that enhances the flavor.

It is only in the past fifteen years or so that grilling and vegetables have become almost synonymous. This traditionally outdoor method of cooking has changed the face of American cuisine. There are restaurants known especially for their grilling capabilities and grilled veggies have become the side dish of choice. Grilling is now a choice for the indoor home cook. You can buy cook-tops and stoves with grill sections that allow indoor grilling as long as the venting system vents outdoors, a very important safety feature one must not ignore.

The traditional grilling season, summer, has now been joined by spring, autumn, and in some cases winter. The main difference in winter grilling is that the cooking time might have to be extended depending on the outdoor temperature. The colder weather tends to cool off the surface of the barbecue requiring it to work a bit harder to maintain the heat. The chilly chef has to change his gear and wear an apron over a parka as opposed to over a bathing suit!

GRILLED
VEGETABLE PLATTER

(1) Drizzle some olive oil onto your serving platter.

(2) Arrange the veggies on the serving platter, tuck the garlic slices in between. (Rule of thumb here is to start with a layer of eggplant slices, add the zucchini slices on spoke-like fashion between the eggplant. Add the pepper, alternating colors, and top with carrot slices in the same manner.

(3) Sprinkle with some salt and pepper to taste and drizzle on more olive oil.

(4) Serve the same day or chill to serve the next day. The flavor is much better if served at room temperature so allow the platter to cool down or come to room temperature as befits the occasion.

 INGREDIENTS

Carrots: scraped, cut lengthwise 1/4-inch thick, coated with oil. Grill 10 minutes on each side.

Eggplant: cut lengthwise, 1/4-1/2-inch thick or cut into 1/4-1/2-inch thick circles, coat with oil. Grill 7-10 minutes each side.

Fennel: Remove the top, fuzzy portion of the fennel leaving just the bulb with about 2-3 inches of stem. Cut the bulb into quarters, coat with oil and grill on all sides. Grill 20-30 minutes.

Mushrooms: Wild or Portobello; remove and discard stem. Brush with oil. Grill 15 minutes on each side. Domestic; trim stem, brush with oil. Grill 7 minutes each side.

Onions: medium to large, peeled, cut in half horizontally. Cut bottoms slightly to form a flat surface, coat with oil. Grill 15 minutes on each side depending on size of the onion.

Peppers: green, red, yellow, or any color of your choice. Cut lengthwise into halves or quarters, Seed and coat lightly with corn oil. Grill 10 minutes each side.

Potatoes: white and sweet: medium to large baking, cut lengthwise into 1/4-1/2-inch thick long or circular slices; coat with oil. Grill 15-20 minutes each side.

Tomatoes: Tomatoes should be medium-ripe, not too soft. Slice in half horizontally and brush top and bottom with oil. Sprinkle fresh herbs on top. Grill on skin side only until skin appears grilled but tomato is still firm, about 10 minutes.

Zucchini: cut lengthwise, 1/4-1/2-inch thick; coat with oil. Grill 7-10 minutes each side.

NOTE: *All items should be brushed with a light coating of oil before being placed on the grill. For extra flavoring dried herbs of choice can be laid on the grill itself with the vegetable on top of the herbs.*

TO SERVE

Have at the ready the grilled veggies, and a large attractive serving platter
4-6 large cloves of garlic, sliced
extra olive oil or specialty flavored olive oil (see Basil Oil, page 35)
salt and pepper
herbs of your choice, fresh or dried
fresh herbs to sprinkle and garnish

NOTE: *Included here are the major vegetables used for grilling. Vegetables that take longer to cook like potatoes, onions, and carrots should start out on the outer edges of the grill or on a raised rack over the grill. After 10 minutes they should be placed directly on the grill for further cooking and grill marks. Select fresh seasonal vegetables. If necessary, cut them the day before and keep well wrapped and chilled.*

SERVES 6-8

LAZY DAY VEGETABLE SOUP
WITH MARROW BALLS

(1) Heat the cooking oil in a large (6-quart) pot and add the bones and the beef shank. Brown lightly on all sides over medium heat. Add the water, spices, 1 teaspoon of salt and 1/2 teaspoon of pepper, the soaked dried beans, barley, and parsley sprigs. Simmer together for 1 hour. Remove the large knuckle bone.

(2) Add all of the vegetables except the peas, corn, and tomatoes. Simmer another hour. Remove parsley sprigs, bones, spice bag, and taste for seasonings. Add more salt and pepper if needed.

(3) Add the corn, peas, and tomatoes; simmer about 10 minutes. Your taste buds now become crucial. Does the soup need a flavor boost or is it to your taste? You can add flavor by dissolving a beef bouillon cube in the liquid. You can also add half a can of condensed cream of tomato soup or a few flakes of hot pepper. However, with all the ingredients included, your soup should be just delicious. You can make the marrow balls while the soup is cooking.

NOTE: *Try to keep a package of shin (also called shank) beef in the freezer along with some marrow bones and knuckle bones so when the first snow falls you can relax, watch the snow accumulate and spend the morning preparing this slow cooking, soul satisfying meal-in-one soup. A loaf of homemade bread is an especially delicious accompaniment.*

INGREDIENTS

1 1/2 pounds of beef shank (sometimes called shin beef)

About 1 pound of marrow and knuckle bones; remove 2 tablespoons of the fresh marrow from the bones with a small spoon and set aside, refrigerated, to be used later for the marrow balls (see page 102)

1 tablespoon of cooking oil

7 cups of water

1 teaspoon of pickling spice, 6 peppercorns and 1 large bay leaf tied in a cheesecloth bag or placed in a stainless steel tea ball

salt and pepper to taste

3 large sprigs of parsley

1/2 cup of mixed dried beans or lentils, quick soaked; follow package instructions

1/2 cup of pearl barley, rinsed and soaked (while meat browns)

1 medium leek, well washed, quartered and thinly sliced

1 medium onion, about 4 ounces, diced small

1 small white turnip, about 4 ounces, peeled and diced small

2 small or 1 large parsnip, 6-7 ounces, peeled and diced small

2-3 carrots, 6-7 ounces, peeled and diced small

2-3 stalks of celery, diced small

1/2 cup of baby lima beans (can use frozen)

1/4 pound of fresh green beans, cleaned and cut into 1/2-inch pieces

1/2 cup of peas

1/2 cup of corn kernels

1 or 2 tomatoes

1/4 cup of chopped parsley for garnish

SERVES 8-10

MARROW BALLS

(1) Combine marrow, butter, eggs, salt, pepper, nutmeg, crumbs, and baking powder in a bowl and beat until smooth, using enough cracker crumbs to hold the mixture together.

(2) Form into marble sized balls. Wetting the hands keep the mixture from sticking.

(3) Cook in simmering broth or water 10-15 minutes. If cooking separately in water, lift out with a slotted spoon when finished and add to soup as you serve it. Recipe makes about 32 balls. Allow about 4 per person.

NOTE: These marble-sized little dumplings go perfectly with the Lazy Day Vegetable Soup on the preceding page. They're a cousin of matzo balls and they can be frozen.

 INGREDIENTS

2 tablespoons of fresh marrow, strained through a sieve
1 tablespoon of butter
3 eggs, beaten lightly
1/2 teaspoon of salt
dash of white pepper
1/8 teaspoon of freshly grated nutmeg
About 1 cup of fine cracker or bread crumbs
1/2 teaspoon of baking powder
broth or water for cooking

MAKES 32 BALLS

INDEX

Traditional Country Life Recipe Books from
BRICK TOWER PRESS

Other titles in this series:

American Chef's Companion
Chocolate Companion
Fresh Herb Companion
Thanksgiving Cookery
Victorian Christmas Cookery
Apple Companion
Pumpkin Companion
Soups, Stews & Chowders
Fresh Bread Companion
Sandwich Companion

Forthcoming titles:

Zucchini Companion
Cranberry Companion
Pie Companion
Ice Cream: A Cook's History of Cold Comfort

MAIL ORDER AND GENERAL INFORMATION
Many of our titles are carried by your local book store or gift and museum shop. If they do not already carry our line please ask them to write us for information.

If you are unable to purchase our titles from your local shop, call or write to us. Our titles are available through mail order. Just send us a check or money order for $9.95 per title with $1.50 postage (shipping is free with 3 or more assorted copies) to the address below or call us Monday through Friday, 9 AM to 5PM, EST. We accept Visa, Mastercard, and American Express cards.

For sales, editorial information, subsidiary rights information or a catalog, please write or phone or e-mail to
Brick Tower Press
1230 Park Avenue
New York, NY 10128, US
Sales: 1-800-68-BRICK
Tel: 212-427-7139 Fax: 212-860-8852
www.BrickTowerPress.com
email: bricktower@aol.com.

For sales in the UK and Europe please contact our distributor,
Gazelle Book Services
Falcon House, Queens Square
Lancaster, LA1 1RN, UK
Tel: (01524) 68765 Fax: (01524) 63232
email: gazelle4go@aol.com.

For Australian and New Zealand sales please contact
INT Press Distribution Pyt. Ltd.
386 Mt. Alexander Road
Ascot Vale, VIC 3032, Australia
Tel: 61-3-9326 2416 Fax: 61-3-9326 2413
email: sales@intpress.com.au.